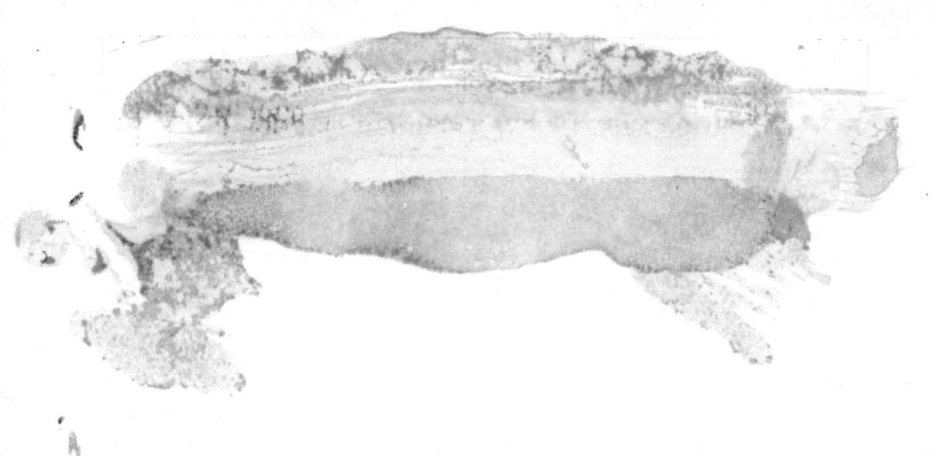

The Economics of Poverty

Introduction to Economics Series

Kenyon A. Knopf, *Editor*

ECONOMIC DEVELOPMENT AND GROWTH
Robert E. Baldwin

THE ECONOMICS OF POVERTY
Alan B. Batchelder

NATIONAL INCOME AND EMPLOYMENT ANALYSIS
Arnold Collery

THE MARKET SYSTEM
Robert H. Haveman and Kenyon A. Knopf

INTERNATIONAL ECONOMIC PROBLEMS
James C. Ingram

WELFARE AND PLANNING: AN ANALYSIS OF
    CAPITALISM VERSUS SOCIALISM
Heinz Köhler

TOWARD ECONOMIC STABILITY
Maurice W. Lee

CASE STUDIES IN AMERICAN INDUSTRY
Leonard W. Weiss

The Economics of Poverty

ALAN B. BATCHELDER
Kenyon College

John Wiley & Sons, Inc. New York · London · Sydney

To Mary Hutchins Batchelder
and William G. Batchelder, Sr.,
still teaching
"Seek truth, then act with justice."

Introduction to Economics Series

Teachers of introductory economics seem to agree on the impracticality of presenting a comprehensive survey of economics to freshmen or sophomores. Many of them believe there is a need for some alternative which provides a solid core of principles while permitting an instructor to introduce a select set of problems and applied ideas. This series attempts to fill that need and also to give the interested layman a set of self-contained books that he can absorb with interest and profit, without assistance.

By offering greater flexibility in the choice of topics for study, these books represent a more realistic and reasonable approach to teaching economics than most of the large, catchall textbooks. With separate volumes and different authors for each topic, the instructor is not as tied to a single track as in the omnibus introductory economics text.

Underlying the series is the pedagogical premise that students should be introduced to economics by learning how economists think about economic problems. Thus the concepts and relationships of elementary economics are presented to the student in conjunction with a few economic problems. An approach of this kind offers a good beginning to the student who intends to move on to advanced work and furnishes a clearer understanding for those whose study of economics is limited to an introductory exposure. Teachers and students alike should find the books helpful and stimulating.

Kenyon A. Knopf, Editor

Preface

This book is about the people who live in poverty in America in the 1960's. Many of us, for a variety of reasons, are impelled to learn all we can about poverty. Now, in 1966, tens of millions of Americans are poor. Most Americans are not poor, but the nonpoor are inextricably involved with the poor because no taxpayer can avoid paying a portion of the costs that poverty imposes. Both government and private programs attempt to heal or hide poverty. These programs consume tens of billions of dollars each year. No American voter can escape the political issues that the programs raise either at the state, city, or federal levels. To be an informed voter, we must have a knowledge of the issues at stake when we go to the polls. If we seek knowledge in order to make policy decisions concerning government or private programs that affect poverty—or if we simply want to know for the sake of knowing—this book may help because it describes the American situation.

Never before have so many people had so much. The physical possessions of the typical American are unprecedented in both number and variety. But every American's income is not high; nor is every American's income rising. This book deals with the reasons for this disparity. We focus upon the dollar incomes of people. Our emphasis upon money raises this fundamental question regarding our basic assumptions: Are spiritual values to be sacrificed before the golden calf of materialism? The premises below explain why they will not be sacrificed.

I am an economist. I have tried to assemble evidence and to provide an analysis that is as accurate as the latest knowledge permits. Yet, underlying my analysis, there are premises and biases common to American economists. These premises and biases should be kept in mind by the reader.

American economists quarrel over many issues, but they agree that the Good Society is one in which the range of choice open to individuals widens each year. The Good Society, while enforcing rules that set limits upon the injuries and inconveniences that one individual may inflict upon another, provides its members with a constantly expanding range of choice in ideas, movement, occupation, and consumption. American economists agree that democracy is the best form of government to provide growing freedom to Americans.

These economists, favoring wide choice of products, stores, jobs, and employers, advocate two principles of organization for the American economy. First, they suggest that farms, mines, factories, and stores should be privately owned. Second, they maintain that for every product there should be many producers and sellers competing for a share of the market and many buyers competing for a share of each product.

The most obvious connection between competitive private ownership and expanding freedom of choice is that government ownership and private monopoly (or near monopoly) severely restrict the range of choice of buyers, sellers, and job seekers. Private ownership and many producers provide a wide range of choices. Moreover, a private or government monopolist can ignore means to cut costs, since he can pass along high costs to the consumers who have nowhere else to go to buy. The competitor, in contrast, must constantly fear that other businesses will take away his market by improving the product or by cutting costs and then prices. Thus, competitive private ownership presses every businessman to be as considerate of customers as is possible and as efficient as he can be. This efficiency maximizes output, and maximum output provides buyers with a maximum range of choice among goods and services.

However, as I have already suggested, not all Americans enjoy a growing freedom. The amount of money that a man has largely affects the range of choices that are open to him. A poor man is therefore limited in his freedom. Consequently, among the causes that limit freedom of choice, poverty is a primary one. Our study investigates the characteristics, causes, and cures of American poverty.

Many discussions of poverty are interlaced with slogans—with crusading and countercrusading battle cries. I made an effort, in writing this book, to keep myself out of the battle and to avoid both the language and attitudes of the crusaders and countercrusaders. Some chapters are devoted to subjects that spark controversy—such as aid to dependent children, the Job Corps, the negative income tax, the progressive income tax, and the regressive property tax; but I have limited myself (I hope) to a dispassionate description and analysis of existing conditions and of the probable consequences of various changes advocated by influential groups. With respect to the controversial questions, each person should form his own judgments based on the available facts and his personal value system.

The first four chapters describe the character and extent of poverty in America. The next four chapters analyze the causes of American poverty. Chapter 9 describes programs that transfer money from the nonpoor to the poor. Chapter 10 analyzes programs designed to help the poor to work their way out of poverty. The last chapter describes the character of many of the choices affecting poverty that most of us will be called upon to make at times during our lives. Every chapter is presented within the context of two assumptions: American society should provide individuals with a growing range of choice; and the American economy should remain, as it is today, with most production in the hands of private competitive businesses.

I am intellectually indebted to many friends, teachers, students, and authors. I would like to express particular thanks to Professors Blaine E. Grimes of Ohio Wesleyan University, Eugene Clark of Washington State University, Alexander Gerschenkron of Harvard University, Paul Craig of The Ohio State University, and Carl Brehm, Paul Titus, and Paul Trescott of Kenyon College; their inspiration and counsel have been of inestimable value. Harold Friedt gave generously of his time in reading the manuscript, and his advice has greatly improved the quality of this book.

Kenyon A. Knopf and John P. Young of John Wiley and Sons originally conceived the idea of such a book as a useful tool of analysis for college students and laymen. Arthur W. Hepner of John Wiley and Sons read the entire manuscript and, by his wisdom, wit, and delightful mastery of English, provided counsel that transformed the prose into a style far more fluent than I could have offered without his aid. My wife, Joan, while caring for Bruce, David, Michael, and Ann, gave advice and moral support, bore the burden of half of the typing, and protected me from my children and my children from me during periods of creative stress. Mrs. Hope Weir did an excellent job in typing half of the manuscript. Mrs. Maryanne Stewart expertly compiled the index that concludes this book.

The virtues of this book, whatever they may be, place me under obligation to many people in many places. But its defects are mine alone.

ALAN B. BATCHELDER

Contents

PART *I*

POVERTY: WHAT IS IT?

1

Where to Draw the Line

The purpose of this book is to provide a perspective on American poverty. As a first step, it is necessary to count the number of Americans who are poor. To count the poor, we must be able to distinguish between poor and nonpoor. To do this requires a definition of poverty that easily permits the distinction. We cannot translate the dictionary definition into dollars and cents. Dictionaries refer vaguely to "insufficiency of means" but do not provide dollar-and-cents criteria. We need a count based on such criteria, which can be used with available statistics.

Ideally, poverty should be defined in terms of the amount of money available to a family as compared with the money it needs to spend during a given year. Compliance with this definition, when counting the nation's poor, necessitates complete information regarding *every* family's assets, its access to credit, its annual earned income (wages, salaries, interest, profits) and unearned income (pensions, unemployment compensation, welfare payments), and its cash-expenditure needs. In most cases, because of limited availability of dollar data, only figures on earned *and* unearned cash income are available. Hence, counts of the poor must be based on a cash-income criterion alone. This criterion might indicate, for example, that a family with an annual cash income of $2999 or less is poor, while a family with an annual cash income of $3000 or more is not poor.

The cash-income criterion of need has proved useful but is difficult to establish. What cash income will barely satisfy minimum needs? One man's opinion of need is likely to differ from *every* other man's opinion. At the end of this chapter, we shall return to the difficulties caused by the diversity of opinion regarding income needs. Meanwhile let us consider the associated problems that must be resolved if we are to understand the meaning of a census of poor Americans.

I. INCOME VERSUS ASSETS

First, how important are assets as distinct from income? Income (a flow) is what a family takes in between the first and last days of a year. Assets (a stock) is how much a family owns on the last (or first) day of a year. Assets include property, stocks, bonds, bank accounts and, for some people who distrust banks, a cigar box or mattress stuffed with dollar bills. A family without any assets on January 1 can live quite comfortably during the year if its income is ample. A family with *no* income but with large assets can also live quite comfortably by selling a portion of its assets each month during the year.

Sometimes we use only income criteria when counting the poor. Consequently, some families with low or negative incomes will be counted as poor even though they possess large assets. How much error will this limitation introduce into the count? Presumably, most people with large assets receive large incomes in the form of profits, rent, or interest. Thus, the income criterion will include as poor only a few families with large assets, but this criterion will introduce error whenever families with large assets have low or negative incomes. Chapter 3 introduces some statistical data regarding family assets, and the count of the poor in that chapter is adjusted to reflect the assets' importance.

In general, there is little information available regarding the assets or the access to credit of individual families. However, assets and credit accessibility derive in large part from past income, and some statistics have been collected on family income for periods of longer than one year. These statistics merit consideration. For example, a family with an income of $10,000 one year may, because of illness or unemployment, drop to an income of $2000 the following year. During the second year, this family would have more assets and greater access to credit than a family with an income of $2000 for two consecutive years. If the income line for counting poor families were changed from $3000 for one year to $6000 for two years, in the second year many families with large assets and ready access to credit but temporarily low income would not be counted with the families that experienced low income as a chronic phenomenon.

The Department of Commerce, experimenting with a poverty criterion of a $6000 family income for two years, has concluded that "a poverty criterion based on a two-year income average of $3000 yields nearly as many low-income families as is indicated by the one-year" family-income criterion.[1] Even though the use of the two-year criterion has little effect on the total number of families counted as poor, it would be more accurate than the one-year criterion. The two-year criterion would exclude from the count of the poor all famlies like the one with an income of $2000 in one year but an income of $10,000 in the preceding year, and would count as poor all families with incomes of $3400 in one year and $2400 in the other year. If information regarding two-year (or three- or four-year) family income becomes available on a national basis, the need to know about assets will become less pressing, and the count of the American poor will be improved. As yet this information is not available.

II. MONEY INCOME VERSUS INCOME IN KIND

Second, some American families receive all of their income in cash, whereas others receive some income in cash and some in kind. "Income in kind" refers to goods and services that individuals receive either from gardens or homes they own or from an employer in addition to cash wages. For example, servants may receive room and board as part of their pay.

---

[1] *Economic Report of the President: 1965,* U.S. Government Printing Office, Washington, 1965, p. 165.

Room and board are income in kind. Many families cultivate vegetable gardens; the produce of such gardens is income in kind. Some people own clear title to their homes; the use of the house is income in kind.

For families receiving all of their income in cash, money income and total income are the same thing. The total income of people with income in kind is equal to money income *plus* the money value of the goods and services received as income in kind, and their cash needs are lessened by the value of the income in kind. The ideas involved in this discussion are easy to describe. The difficulty arises when we try to obtain statistics showing the money value of goods and services received as income in kind.

We can imagine two cases: A man, 35, with a wife and two children, is in poor health and works only part time. A second man, 35, also has a wife and two children, is in poor health, and works only part time. Both families had cash incomes of $2400 last year. In short, both families are the same in every respect except: the first lives in the country and owns a clear title to his home, whereas the second family lives in the city and pays rent for its home (its position would be the same if the husband were making payments on a 25-year mortgage). Because its house is paid for, the first family is always better off than the second family. It is better off by the amount of income in kind that it receives from its house. The difference between the two families would be even greater if the first family cultivated a vegetable garden. Such differences in real income can exist despite the identical cash incomes received by the two families.

To calculate the total income of families living in their own homes or receiving income in kind in other forms, we must estimate the money value of the income in kind. For any one case, these values are easily estimated, but our purposes require statistics for the country as a whole. These statistics are essential for comparisons between urban residents who receive relatively little income in kind and rural residents who receive relatively large amounts. In Chapter 3, we estimate the impact of the urban-rural difference in income in kind but omit the income in kind of urban families from our calculations. This omission is unavoidable because of the limitations of present statistical technique. The Department of Commerce once published estimates of the value of income in kind received by groups of urban and rural families but ceased publication of them when convinced that the figures were inaccurate. Reliable figures may become available in the future. If so, the count of both the farm and the nonfarm poor will improve.

III. SIZE OF FAMILY

Third, one husband is 38, married, and has 11 children, the oldest 16 years, the youngest 11 months; his wife is again pregnant. Another husband is 68, his wife is 67; they have no children. Both families rent their homes. The 13-member family had a cash income of $3250 last year. The two-member family had a cash income of $2800.

Suppose we decide to use $3000 in cash income as the dividing line between poor and nonpoor. That is to say, we label a family poor if its annual cash income is less than $3000 and nonpoor if its annual cash income is $3000 or more. Applying this criterion to the two families, we would call the former ($250 income per person) nonpoor and the latter ($1400 income per person) poor.

Many counts of the number of people living in poverty use a single cash-income figure to distinguish poor from nonpoor without allowing for family size. The results of this procedure are sometimes as bizarre as those of the foregoing example. Frequently they are less bizarre but still unsatisfactory.

Chapter 3 shows that poverty counts that take family size into consideration will designate as poor many more families with numerous children than will a flat $3000 income figure. Conversely, any count of the poor that does not allow for family size will underestimate the number of large families that are poor.

IV. AGE, LOCATION, HEALTH

Finally, a man of 70 will usually eat less than a man of 30. A family living in St. Augustine, Florida, will have lower insulation and heating costs than a family living in a house in northern Minnesota. A diabetic must pay more for food and insulin; an invalid must pay more for personal care than a person in good health. If American families are classified as poor or nonpoor on the basis of a cash-income criterion that makes no allowance for the age, location, or health of family members, the final count must be inaccurate. How serious such inaccuracies are is largely a matter of conjecture since, in most cases, we lack statistical data for measuring the inaccuracies. In Chapter 3, an allowance is made for age, but there are no statistics that allow for either location or health.

V. DIVERSITY OF OPINION AND
THE USE OF STATISTICS

Whether poverty is viewed as a national or a regional problem, a count of the poor is required to measure the problem's size, and a poverty line is needed to give policy makers and observers a clear view of the threshold over which every family must pass if poverty is to be eliminated in the United States. According to the dictionaries, poverty means "not enough resources to meet essential needs." To count the poor we must draw a firm dollar line at the point at which a family's money resources exactly meet its essential money needs.

If all essential money needs were met there would be no poverty. But what are essential needs? This is a matter of opinion regarding which honest men differ. Each person sets his own dollar line for essential needs. This diversity of opinion complicates but does not prevent general use of the statistical poverty counts now available.

Man 1 may establish a particular dollar resource line as his judgment of a family's essential money needs and, on that basis, may count the number of people living in poverty. Man 2 may use this count even though his idea of essential need differs from that of Man 1. If Man 2 considers Man 1's idea of essential needs to be unreasonably low, Man 2 can make an upward adjustment in Man 1's count of the poor. Conversely, if Man 2 considers Man 1's notion of essential needs unreasonably high, Man 2 can make a downward adjustment in Man 1's count of the poor. By making appropriate allowances, persons of different judgments can use the same basic set of figures.

VI. SUMMARY

This chapter has provided a perspective on the count of the number of poor Americans. Perspective derives from recognition that available family-need and family-resource data are incomplete and that universal agreement upon essential money needs is out of the question. Given this perspective, we see that existing counts of the poor are without authority but are consistently honest in light of the resource data available and some individual's or group's subjective definition of the dollar resource line between poverty and nonpoverty. We see further that any individual can use someone else's poverty count by recognizing its limitations and appropriately making adjustments to his own opinions and needs.

The next chapter counts the American poor on the basis of a single simple criterion; Chapter 3 counts the poor according to more sophisticated criteria. The counts obtained need not be accepted as final but can be used by anyone willing to make suitable adjustments to them.

PART *II*

HOW MANY POOR?

2

Poverty in America in 1959: The Simple Count

How many Americans are poor? Of the poor, how many live in the North, West, or South? How many live in Mississippi, in the San Francisco metropolitan area, in Cook County, Ill., in Boise, Idaho? How many are children, how many elderly? How many belong to minority groups? The preceding chapter surveyed the problems associated with attempts to count the poor. This chapter provides a sufficiently detailed count to permit specific answers to the foregoing questions and to many others regarding an enumeration of the poor.

I. THE IMPORTANCE OF NUMBERS

Personal decisions and public policy rest upon perspective, which must be accurate if the decisions and the policy are to achieve their intended results. Perspective involves considerations of both analysis and numbers. Economic analysis necessitates the arranging of economic elements into a tight, logical sequence of cause and effect. Subsequent chapters develop this analysis of answers to these questions: (1) Why are some Americans poor? (2) What are the effects of various policies designed to help the poor or to help the poor help themselves? Our analysis will generally be independent of the numbers presented here and will be as valid for 10 thousand poor as for 10 million or 100 million. Yet, numbers are important.

To make decisions, we must count the number of poor—both the total and subtotal. This count will delineate the size and character of the poverty problem. It will identify the point at which there would be no more poor, where the poverty problem would disappear, and where the individuals engaged in fighting poverty would be freed to direct their energies elsewhere.

The United States Constitution requires that a census of population be taken every 10 years so that the seats in the House of Representatives can be allocated among the States in proportion to their populations. A new census has been taken in every tenth year since the first one in 1790, and the most recent one was in April 1960. Each of these has attempted to reach every American.

A complete census is expensive; the 1960 census cost $128 million. However, governments (state, local, and Federal) and businesses often urgently need census information that is as current as the problems that legislators and businesses face. To satisfy these needs by relatively inexpensive means, the Bureau of the Census, soon after the Second World War, began to conduct a monthly current population survey. The Current Population Survey sends interviewers to approximately 35 thousand homes each month of each year. The homes are changed every three months, but all are selected so that, as a group, they typify the entire nation.

From each month's sample, generalizations are extended to the entire population. The techniques of mathematical statistics provide users of the data with precise measures of the reliability of these generalizations. Among the diverse information collected by the Census Bureau in the 1960 decennial census and in the monthly surveys, certain questions and answers help to provide a count of the poor. In each home, the census interviewer might ask, "Are you a poor family?" From this question and the answers it provokes, we might easily obtain the statistics needed. The affirmative replies would supply the number of poor families—that is, poor by their own testimony. Obviously the question is not asked. Moreover, the question of whether we could trust such testimony is moot.

Interviewers could ask questions regarding cash income, income in kind, assets, and all the aspects of need relevant to the identification of poverty. They do not ask all of these questions, but they do ask about the number in each family and about the age, sex, and employment status of each member. They also ask how much, if anything, each member of the family received in cash income during the preceding year.

The required count of poverty will have to be based on the answers to the questions asked. The questions regarding income are phrased in the following manner:

P32. How much did this person earn in 1959 in wages, salary, commissions, or tips from all jobs (before deductions for taxes, bonds, dues, or other items)? (Enter amount or check "None." If exact figure not known, give best estimate.)

$_____.00 or None □

P33. How much did he earn in 1959 in profits or fees from working in his own business, professional practice, partnership, or farm (net income after business expenses)? (Enter amount or check "None." If exact figure not known, give best estimate. If business or farm lost money, write "Loss" after amount.)

$_____.00 or None □

P34. Last year (1959), did this person receive any income from:
Social security?
Pensions?
Veteran's payments?
Rent (minus expenses)?
Interest or dividends?
Unemployment insurance?
Welfare payments?
Any other source not already entered?
Yes □   No □
What is the amount he received from these sources in 1959? (If exact figure not known, give best estimate.)

$_____.00

Information is requested of all persons 14 years of age and older in the households reached by the census staff. Receipts from the following sources are not included as income: money received from the sale of property, unless received as the net income of a person in the business of selling such property; money borrowed; withdrawals of bank deposits; tax refunds; gifts and lump-sum inheritances or insurance benefits; the value of income in kind, such as free living quarters or food produced and consumed in the home. The term annual income as used in this book refers to the total amounts indicated in the answers to all three income questions.

According to the Census Bureau, a family consists of two or more persons living in the same household who are related to each other by blood, marriage, or adoption; all persons living in one household who are related to each other are regarded as one family. The annual income of a family is found by totaling the answers to each of the three income questions given by each family member 14 years old or over.

How good and how reliable are these figures? Intensive spot checks against factory pay records and income tax returns and reinterviews by the Census Bureau have uncovered many errors, but overstatements virtually balance understatements by members of families with low incomes. Interest and dividend payments are under-reported by about 10%, but reports of wages and salaries are generally accurate. Individual reports are often wrong, but the averages are usually valid. In short, the annual cash income data are reliable for families with low incomes.

The Census Bureau feeds these income figures into its computers and could instruct the machines to "count the number of families with an income . . ." of $1000, the number with an income of $1001, the number with an income of $1002, etc. If the Bureau finished the instructions this way, the final report would fill a table containing several million rows of figures, one for every different dollar of income. Instead, the Bureau commands the machine to "count the number of families with an income of $999 or less, the number with an income between $1000 and $1999 inclusive, the number with an income between $2000 and $2999 inclusive. . . ." The instructions continue, producing such results as those shown for 1959 in Table 2-1.

II. THE SIMPLE METHOD TO COUNT THE
NUMBER OF POOR FAMILIES IN 1959

Chapter 1 listed the statistics necessary for a precise count of poverty. Lacking these data we must rely on the available sta-

Table 2-1 Number and Percent of Families with 1959 Incomes within Specific Ranges; For the Entire United States and for Selected Geographic Areas (1000s)

							Region						
Income Range (Total)	United States		The South		Mississippi		San Francisco Metropolitan Area		Cook County		Boise	
	Number	Per-cent	Number	Per-cent	Number	Per-cent	Number	Per-cent	Number	Per-cent	Number	Per-cent
Total with income	45,130	100.0	13,509	100.0	501	100.0	705	100.0	1314	100.0	9.0	100.0
Under $1000	2,513	5.6	1302	9.6	98	19.6	20	2.8	37	2.8	0.3	2.9
$1000 to $1999	3374	7.5	1584	11.7	90	18.0	28	4.0	49	3.7	0.6	7.0
$2000 to 2999	3764	8.3	1584	11.7	70	14.0	35	5.0	59	4.5	0.7	7.3
$3000 to $3999	4283	9.5	1581	11.7	56	11.2	44	6.3	74	5.6	0.9	10.1
$4000 to $4999	4958	11.0	1512	11.2	47	9.4	56	8.0	102	7.8	1.1	11.9
$5000 to $9999	19,444	43.1	4563	33.8	114	22.7	350	49.5	656	49.9	4.0	44.5
$10,000 to $14,999	4728	10.5	949	7.0	18	3.6	119	16.9	231	17.6	1.1	11.7
$15,000 and over	2066	4.6	434	3.2	8	1.6	53	7.5	106	8.1	0.4	4.6

Source. U.S. Bureau of the Census. *U.S. Census of Population: 1960. United States Summary*, Table 224; *Mississippi*, Table 139; *California*, Table 139; *Illinois*, Table 86; and *Iowa*, Table 86, U.S. Government Printing Office, Washington, D.C., 1963.

tistics of cash income. Equating poverty with low cash income, we can obtain a count of the poor by drawing a horizontal line across Table 2-1 at the proper level. All families below this line can be designated "not poor," and all above the line can be identified as "poor." This is the simple method of counting the number of poor families.

The problem is where to draw the line. It can be drawn between $999 and $1000, between $1999 and $2000, or between $3999 and $4000. There are several possibilities. Low-income families spend about one third of their income on food; the other two thirds goes for housing, clothing, transportation, social insurance taxes, private insurance (if any), and other items (if any). From this practice, there follow these choices for the poverty line for a family of four persons:

The Line Between (Dollars)	Total Income per Week (Dollars)	Spent on Food Each Month (Dollars)	(Cents) Spent per Meal per Person
999–1000	19.23	27.78	7.6
1999–2000	38.47	55.56	15.2
2999–3000	57.70	83.34	22.8
3999–4000	76.94	111.12	30.4

Each individual will have his own preference of where the line should lie. If the Census Bureau had prepared the million-line family-income report showing the number of families receiving each of the possible dollar income totals, there would be a far wider range of choice. For example, one could then define poor families as those with cash income below $2813— or as those with cash income below $3472. But the Bureau publishes census data only for the classes shown in Table 2-1. Using this data, the line distinguishing poor from nonpoor must be drawn between two of these classes.

In this chapter we draw the line between $2999 and $3000. The four-person family receiving $3000 a year and able to spend 22.8¢ per person per meal on food will be classified as *not* poor. A family with a smaller income, with a $2999 income, for example, will be classified as poor, whether this family contains two persons or ten, whether it is a farm or a nonfarm family.

The $2999 maximum is used here because most government reports and many private studies in recent years have used this annual income figure to distinguish between poor and non-poor families. The rationale for this particular poverty line derives (1) from the discovery that low-income families spend one third of their income on food, (2) from willingness to use a family of four as the typical American family (average family size was 3.65 in 1960), and (3) from the Department of Agriculture calculation that in 1959 the cost of minimally nutritional meals averaged about 22.8¢ per person in a family of two adults and two children. For such a family, barely adequate food costs would average $2.736 a day; other costs would average $5.472 a day; and total cash needs for a 365-day year would be ($5.472 + $2.736) × 365 = $2,995.92 a year.

For this four-person family, a $2999 poverty criterion would provide $3 more than the nutritional minimum. In the regions mentioned in Table 2-1 the 1959 count of poverty, on the basis of the $2999 criterion, would be as follows.

9,651,000 families in the United States
4,470,000 families in the South
258,000 families in Mississippi
83,000 families in metropolitan San Francisco
145,000 families in Cook County
1600 families in Boise

Anyone dissatisfied with the poverty line based on a per person–per meal food cost of 22.8¢ may increase the poverty count by raising the income level at which the line is drawn or reduce the count by lowering the income level at which the line is drawn. If an individual were thus moved, he could wipe out poverty by uninhibited reduction in the level of the poverty line.

This definition of poverty based on the 1959 cash income classes of Table 2-1 is useful to the general public because it can be used by any individual to determine the number of poor families in his own geographic region, state, standard metropolitan statistical area (counties containing and econom-

ically tied to a large city), county, or city. He need only turn
to the appropriate page in the appropriate 1960 census volume to
obtain income statistics for specific geographic areas.[1]

For many people, concern about poverty begins at home.
With the 1960 census statistics, individuals can easily determine
how much poverty there was at home in 1959.

III. CHARACTERISTICS OF THE
HEADS OF POOR FAMILIES

A count of the total number of poor families suggests the size
of the poverty problem. The method used in this chapter has
yielded a count of about 9.7 million poor families in the United
States in 1959. Classifying families according to various characteristics measured in the 1960 census, we can identify seven
mutually exclusive groups among the approximately 9.7 million families with incomes below $3000 in 1959:

3,002,000 with the family head aged 65 or older
1,557,000 with the family head a woman under age 65
  614,000 with the family head a man under age 25
3,011,000 with the family head a man aged 25 to 64 with less
than 9 years of education
  709,000 with the family head a man aged 25 to 64 who dropped
out of high school
   93,000 with the family head a nonwhite man aged 25 to 64
who graduated from high school
  665,000 with the family head a white man aged 25 to 64 who
graduated from high school

Among the 9.7 million poor families, only 665 thousand were
headed by white men aged 25 to 65 with 12 or more years of education. Poverty is relatively rare among families headed by white

---

[1] Detailed national and state data can be found in Tables 224 and 266 of
the volume *U.S. Census of Population: 1960. United States Summary.
Detailed Characteristics.* Detailed standard metropolitan statistical area,
county, and city data can be found in Tables 66, 76, and 86 of the appropriate state volume of *U.S. Census of Population: 1960. General Social
and Economic Characteristics.* Most American libraries, even those of small
towns and small colleges, have copies of these books.

men aged 25 to 64 with at least a high school education. In contrast, poverty is relatively common among families headed by older people, by women, by young men, by poorly educated men, or by nonwhite men. This categorization provides a foretaste of the subject matter of the chapters to come. But first, let us consider a more precise enumeration of those whose resources are inadequate to meet essential needs.

3

Poverty in America in the Sixties: The More Precise Count

The simple method for counting the number of *families* living in poverty employs only one criterion—an annual cash income of $2999. It is an important criterion because of its rationale that for a typical family of four, an income of less than $3000 would not permit a diet satisfying minimal nutritional requirements. Moreover, it has been widely used by officials and commentators, and individuals can use it with 1960 census data to tally the number of poor families in their own region, state, standard metropolitan statistical area, or other political subdivision. But this criterion is weak because it fails to allow for family assets, farm or nonfarm residence (farm families presumably receive income in kind), size of family, or other variables affecting family resources and essential family needs.

To provide a more accurate count of the poor, the United States Social Security Administration, in 1965, formulated new criteria. These criteria allow for farm-nonfarm residence, the sex of the head of the family, the total number in the family, and the number of children under 18 years of age. The criteria do not allow for family assets (stocks, bonds, house) or for variations in family need other than those implied by the variables listed.

The Social Security Administration (SSA) criteria serve more effectively than the single $2999 standard to identify families whose money resources fall short of essential family money needs. Using distinctions based on its four variables, the SSA identified 124 types of family and calculated an appropriate dollar-income poverty line for each.

The calculations began with the assumption that low-income families spent one third of their total income on food, as had been demonstrated empirically. Then, using 1963 prices, the SSA computed the minimum cost of minimally nutritious meals for each of the 124 family classes. For example, a four-person family of father, mother, and two children under 18 was found to require 23.82¢ per person per meal (because food prices rose almost 5% between 1959 and 1963, this figure is higher than the amount mentioned in the last chapter for 1959). It followed that this family would need $2.8584 per day for food and 2 × $2.8584 = $5.7168 per day for all other items: clothing, rent or mortgage payments, utilities and heat, transportation, school supplies and books, home furnishings and supplies, medical care, personal care, and other things. The total figure came to $8.5752 per day. The poverty line for this particular family of four was, therefore, between $3129 ($8.5752 × 365) and $3130. Thus, a family receiving $3130 was classified as not poor and a family receiving $3129 as poor.

A farm family with the same number-age-sex characteristics as the nonfarm family described was assumed to need only 60% of the cash income of the nonfarm family. For the four-person family described, 60% of its $3129 poverty criterion yielded a $1877 criterion for its farm counterpart. (Since completing its calculations, the Social Security Administration has had some afterthoughts suggesting that 70% would be a more accurate adjustment figure.)

The figures $3129 and $1877 were, therefore, the 1963 poverty criteria for two of the 124 classes of family. By similar processes, poverty criteria were calculated for each of the other 122 family classes. Lacking a decennial census in 1964 to yield data on 1963 family incomes, the Social Security Administration relied on a 1964 Current Population Survey to collect data on the 1963 incomes of American families.

Having established the 124 income criteria, the Social Security Administration used them to distinguish between poor and nonpoor in the Current Population Survey and to generalize to all Americans who received incomes during 1963. For perspective, the Social Security Administration further employed the Current Population Survey data to count the number of persons poor by the single $2999 poverty criterion. It did not, however, apply the 124 criteria to the data collected in the 1960 decennial census.

Used with Current Population Survey data only, the SSA's findings suffered a severe limitation. Generalizations can be made from the Survey to the entire United States, but not to states, much less to counties or cities, for the Survey sample of 35 thousand families is too small. Table 3-1 presents the results of alternatively using the simple method and the SSA criteria to count the number of persons living in poverty in the United States. The totals obtained from the two methods differed little, the simple method counting 33.4 million poor Americans and the SSA criteria counting 34.6 million in 1963.

Table 3-1 Americans Living in Poverty in 1963, by Alternative Low-Income Definitions of Poverty (in Millions)

Type of Unit	Total U. S. Population	By the Simple Method		By the 124 Criteria	
		Number	Percent	Number	Percent
Total number of persons:	187.2	33.4	17.8	34.6	18.5
Farm	12.6	4.9	38.9	3.2	25.4
Nonfarm	174.6	28.5	16.3	31.4	18.0
White	165.4			23.9	14.4
Nonwhite	21.8			10.7	49.3
Unattached individuals	11.2	4.9	43.9	4.9	43.9
Members of family units	176.0	28.5	16.2	29.7	16.9
Children under age 18:	68.8	10.8	15.7	15.0	21.9
Farm	4.8	1.8	37.5	1.5	31.2
Nonfarm	64.0	9.0	14.1	13.5	21.1

Source. Social Security Bulletin, Vol. 28, No. 1, January 1965, p. 11, and Vol. 28, No. 7, July 1965, p. 27.

I. UNATTACHED INDIVIDUALS

Before considering the breakdown in Table 3-1, the new term "unattached individuals" in the left-hand column of the table requires explanation. A family, by definition, never has fewer than two persons. Yet some Americans live alone. A man who lives alone in an urban apartment is not a family; neither is a woman who lives alone in a small rented home in the country. Similarly 37 men who rent rooms at a YMCA do not individually or collectively constitute a "family." They are all classified by the Census Bureau as "unattached" or "unrelated" individuals. The latter term is misleading, since each of these people may have many relatives. Both terms mean that such people live alone or in group quarters such as the YMCA. (Prisoners and other institutionalized persons are in another category.)

Unattached individuals were not mentioned in the earlier discussion of 1960 census data because these reports included G.I.'s in barracks and college students in dormitories with the other persons classified as unattached individuals. The presence of the G.I.'s and students rendered the statistics useless for purposes of counting the poor. The Current Population Survey excludes barracks soldiers and sailors and college dormitory residents from its count of unattached individuals.

The Social Security Administration calculates its poverty criteria for unattached individuals as well as for families. The criteria for unattached individuals range from $880 for a woman over the age of 65 living on a farm to $1650 for a man under 65 living in a city. The statistics regarding unattached individuals in the last two columns of Table 3-1 are based on these SSA criteria. Those statistics in the preceding two columns of the table are based on a single poverty criterion between $1499 and $1500 for all unattached individuals. Both the SSA criteria and the $1499 criterion count the same number of unattached individuals, 4,900,000, as having lived in poverty in 1963.

II. A BETTER COUNT

The more successful a poverty count is in identifying persons whose resources are insufficient to meet essential needs, the more effective is the count. The essential needs that would be

met by the SSA poverty income criteria roughly include all
twentieth century minima of conveniences: electric lighting, a
double bed for every two people in a family, a table with enough
chairs and silverware so the entire family can eat together,
transportation to and from work, an indoor flush toilet, cold
and hot water, a refrigerator, and the minimum quantity and
quality of food, medical care, shelter, and clothing required
to yield good health. If every American had this minimum of
goods and services, there would be no poverty in the United
States. Having varied the income criteria of poverty to corre-
spond with the concept of essential money needs for different
kinds of families and unattached individuals, the SSA standards
provide a better count of the poor than the far simpler cash-
income criteria of $2999 for all families and $1499 for all unattached individuals.

A skimming of Table 3-1 discloses the improvements. Some
of the differences between the results of the two methods of
counting the poor merit comment. Under the $2999 criterion,
all families, no matter how small, with incomes below $3000
are poor; all families, no matter how large, with incomes above
$2999 are not poor. The family of two elderly people with an
income of $2900 is counted as poor. The family with thirteen
members and an annual income of $3250 is counted as not
poor. In contrast, the SSA criteria count as not poor small families
of two and three persons with cash incomes below $3000. The
SSA method counts as poor some families with incomes above
$3000 but with 5, 6, 8, 10, or more mouths to feed and bodies
to clothe. By SSA standards, the two-person $2900 income fam-
ily is not poor, whereas the thirteen-person $3,250 income family
is poor.

Counting as not poor many two-person, childless couples
with incomes below $3000, the SSA criteria drop 3 million
family adults from the category of poor, which were included
by the $2999 criterion. The SSA criteria cut from 3.1 million
to 1.5 million the number of poor families headed by a person
aged 65 or older. Counting as poor more large families, though
not all as large as our thirteen-member family, the SSA criteria
identify 1.6 million fewer poor families but an additional 4.2
million needy children than does the single criterion. Because

of the farm-nonfarm differences in poverty criteria for families
and for unattached individuals, the SSA count of the poor includes 1.7 million fewer farm persons and 2.9 million more nonfarm persons than does the simple count of the poor.

III. ADJUSTING THE COUNT

In sum, 34.6 million Americans were poor in 1963 according
to the SSA criteria. No one has suggested that this is the exact
size of the poverty problem in the United States. Each person
may want to adjust the total figure. Several adjustments are
possible.

Both this chapter and the previous one base their counts of
the poor exclusively upon cash income. This method begs the
question, "How many people counted as poor on the basis of
cash income would be regarded *not* poor if cash income *and*
assets were considered?" Aged couples are likelier than young
couples to have large assets. Farmers with a $2500 net income
sometimes have large investments in buildings and equipment.
The simple count of poverty may have included many aged
couples and farmers with $2000 to $2999 income but with large
assets. The SSA criteria drop from the count of poor both the
elderly and small families on farms with incomes between $2000
and $2999. By removing these two groups, the SSA criteria
serve more effectively than the $2999 criterion to exclude families
with large assets.

It would be helpful to know the total assets of every American
family. Although figures are not available for every family,
asset data are available for aged families—the families likeliest
to have large assets. A Social Security Administration survey of
the aged in 1963 investigated the extra spendable income that
elderly people could have each year if they would draw upon
their assets (other than equity in their homes) at a rate calculated actuarially to exhaust these assets over the average years
of life remaining. Under the SSA poverty criteria, these calculations showed that allowance for assets other than homes
would reduce the number of elderly poor by a little less than
10%, from 5.2 to 4.7 million. On the average, young people
have fewer assets than elderly people. There are no statistics,

however, to show the extent to which an allowance for assets would reduce the count of the poor among persons under the age of 65.

A second adjustment might be made for young families with favorable prospects. In 1963, according to SSA criteria, 530 thousand poor families were headed by men under 25. Some of these men were sick, some were high-school dropouts. But some of these men were in college, in graduate school, or in apprenticeship programs. The apprentice carpenter or the candidate for the doctor of philosophy degree are, for most purposes, not part of the poverty problem. An adjustment of between 100 and 200 thousand families might remove from the count all poor young families with glowing prospects.

A third adjustment might be made for the poor people who do not want to change their condition. Some examples appeared when a young doctor in a small town on the Cumberland plateau listened sympathetically to a series of men who came to him and drawled, "Doctor, ahm outa work, but m' family needs doctorin. If you kin help 'em ah'l pay you when ah kin." The doctor replied, "I have six acres to clear, I'll give you a job starting tomorrow at a dollar and a quarter an hour. You use the money any way you like. I'll treat your family, but I know you need money for other things; so you don't have to pay me at all."

Over a period of several months, the doctor told this to 26 men. One of them came to the site the next day accompanied by his entire family, who sat down to watch him work—except his father who ranged round the job giving instructions. After an hour, they all left never to return. One other man came and remained, off and on, for more than a year working in a desultory manner. The other 24 simply disappeared.

Many children leave such families and go to cities. Even fathers of such families sometimes leave their wives and children and go to cities for work, good pay, and slum boarding houses. In the city there are no raccoons, no woods, no great open spaces, no front porches, and no numberless sympathetic relatives and children. Drawn back by land and by blood, many of these outmigrants soon yield to their strong homing instinct, quit their city jobs, and return to their tight, loyal family units with 10 beds in two rooms. Every hand—male and female—

helps with the babies. There is the satisfaction of being on family land with ample space to move, and the most pressing concern is the desire to keep things about the same next year as they are this year.

Given their knowledge of present and prospective alternatives, some poor Americans prefer not to change. They prefer poverty to the movement required to escape poverty. One resident of a timbered Tennessee mountain cove made the point simply when asked why he had come back from Detroit. He answered, "Oh, ah guess ahm OK here."

People who do not want to change may not be part of the poverty problem. Should the SSA count of the problem be adjusted by subtracting all members of such families or by subtracting *only* the adult members of such families? Should any adjustment be made?

IV. THE INCOME DEFICIT

Previous sections have sought a count of the number of poor Americans. There is another way of assessing the magnitude of the poverty problem. This method provides a dollar measure of the size of the problem. The 34.6 million people counted as poor by the SSA criteria had an actual total money income of $17.3 billion in 1963. Had their income been $28.8 billion, then all 34.6 million could have crossed the threshold out of poverty. The $28.8 billion money income required to meet essential money needs was 60% greater than the actual money income received. To this $11.5 billion difference between actual income and minimal nonpoverty income, the Social Security Administration has given the name, the poverty income deficit. If an additional $11.5 billion in money income (1.9% of 1963 gross national product) had been suitably distributed among the 34.6 million people in 1963, there would have been no poverty in the United States in that year.

V. THE INCIDENCE OF POVERTY AMONG INDIVIDUALS

The SSA criteria showed the incidence of poverty to have been especially high among five kinds of individuals. These five categories were: nonwhite children, unattached individuals, nonwhites aged 18 or older, persons aged 65 or older, and farm residents. In 1963, according to the SSA criteria, 21.9% of children under 18 were poor. This is the figure for white and nonwhite children combined. Among white children, the incidence of poverty was relatively low: 15.7%. In sharp contrast, 60% of nonwhite children were poor.

Among whites aged 18 or older, only 13.7% were poor. Among nonwhites aged 18 or older, 40.5% were poor. Among persons aged 65 or over, 30.9% were poor; when allowance was made for assets, this figure was cut to 27.5%. Among farm residents, 25.4% were poor. This relatively high rate prevailed even though the money-income poverty criteria were only 60% as high for farmers as for nonfarmers.

Among unattached individuals, one third of the men and one half of the women were poor. Considering men and women together, 43.9% of all unattached individuals were poor.

The incidence of poverty in the total population provides a base for comparing each of these figures. For the entire population, the incidence of poverty was 18.5%.

VI. THE INCIDENCE OF POVERTY AMONG FAMILIES

The head of each American family bears primary responsibility for earning the money required to support the family. This responsibility is most easily met when the family head is an urban white male between the ages of 25 and 64. Not all American families are headed by urban white men between the ages of 25 and 64. The incidence of poverty is especially high among families headed by nonwhites, by women, by persons under 25, by persons over 64, and by farmers.

Among families headed by nonwhites, 42% were identified as poor in 1963 by the SSA criteria. Only 12% of white families were poor. Among families headed by women, 40% were poor. Only 12% of families headed by men were poor. Among families headed by persons under age 25, 26% were poor. Among families headed by persons over age 64, 24% were poor. Finally, among farm families, 23% were poor. Each of these figures can be compared to the base of 15%, the incidence of poverty in 1963 among all of America's 47.4 million families.

VII. SUMMARY

By estimating the cost of the groceries required to meet minimal nutritional needs, the SSA set out to count the number of poor in America. Calculating food costs, then multiplying by three, the SSA obtained poverty income criteria tailored to fit the needs of different kinds of families and different kinds of unattached individuals. Allowances were made for differences in money income needs resulting from differences in age, sex, and family size, and from the income in kind accruing to people living on farms. Separate criteria of essential money-income need were calculated for 124 different kinds of families and for a dozen categories of unattached individuals.

Though the SSA criteria fail to allow for assets (except as noted below), for differences in health, or for income in earlier years, the enumeration of poverty described in this chapter is more accurate than the enumeration of poverty described in Chapter 2. The SSA criteria count as poor fewer small families, fewer elderly people, fewer farm residents, and 40% more children than do the simple $1499 and $2999 criteria. The total count by the SSA was 34.6 million poor in the United States in 1963.

That count was reduced by 500 thousand elderly people when allowance was made for the assets (except houses) owned by elderly persons. The size of the poverty problem could be cut another several hundred thousand by excluding families headed by young men with low incomes while in graduate work or other training programs leading to assured high incomes in the near future. The count of poverty could be further reduced if one were to exclude from it all families that preferred poverty income living arrangements to any other living arrangements.

Comparing the money income received in 1963 by the 34.6 million poor to the income necessary to move all these people across the threshold out of poverty, the SSA found a difference of $11.5 billion. This $11.5 billion differential was labeled the "poverty income deficit." If the 34.6 million poor had received an additional $11.5 billion (1.9% of 1963 gross national product), poverty would have vanished in the United States in 1963.

Turning to particular groups, the SSA criteria showed the

incidence of poverty to have been particularly high among the following five kinds of individuals: nonwhite children under 18, 59.5%; unattached individuals, 43.9%; nonwhites, 18 and over, 40.5%; persons aged 65 or older, 30.9%; and farm residents, 25.4%. The incidence of poverty among each of these groups can be compared to the 18.5% incidence of poverty for the entire population.

Among the 47.4 million families in America in 1963, 15% were identified as poor by SSA criteria. Among five kinds of families, the incidence of poverty was much higher. These five kinds were the families headed by nonwhites (42% poor), women (40% poor), persons under 25 (26% poor), persons over 64 (24% poor), and farmers (23% poor).

The 34.6 million poor persons comprised 29.7 million members of family groups and 4.9 million unattached individuals. Among the unattached, 59% were age 65 or older. Moreover, of the 4.9 million poor persons there were 3.1 million who did not work during 1963, 600 thousand who worked part of the year, and 1.2 million who worked full time for 50 or more weeks. Of the 29.7 million members of poor families, 15.1 million were under 18, 2.7 million were past 64 (1.5 million of these headed families), 4.3 million were wives under 65 in families headed by a man, and 2 million were other persons aged 18 to 64 in families headed by someone else. These groups totalled 24.1 million. The other 5.6 million were family heads aged 18 to 64; 4 million were men and 1.6 million were women. Of the women, 640 thousand were nonwhite, 960 thousand were white, and 900 thousand did not work. Among the 700 thousand who did work 500 thousand worked part of the year, whereas 200 thousand worked full time. Of the 4 million men aged 18 to 64 heading poor families, 1 million were nonwhite, 3 million were white, and 500 thousand did no work during the year. Among the 3.5 million employed, 1.6 million worked only part of the year, and 1.9 million worked all year.

Chapter 2 emphasized the significance of inferior education as a cause of poverty. The present chapter, frequently reinforced by the evidence of Chapter 2, underscores the association between poverty and old age, youth, color, and the absence from families of male leadership. We have shown that in one eighth of the families headed by women 18 to 64 and in one half of the families led by men 18 to 64, the family head worked full time all year and *still* failed to carry his or her family across the poverty threshold. Among unattached individuals aged 18 to 64, 42% worked full time but remained poor. Most of these long-working, low-income people had received little education.

The following chapters analyze the causes of poverty and the events or programs that may move Americans into or out of poverty. Attention will be focused on the fact that most of the poor are either very young or very old, whereas most of the 18- to 64-year-old poor are either nonwhite, poorly educated, or both.

By way of transition between the preceding statistical section and the forthcoming analytical section, Chapter 4 describes the changes in the incidence and character of poverty that have occurred over past centuries and during recent decades.

4

Through the Years with Poverty

The medieval gentry, when referring to their own offspring, used the Latin word *liberi* (children), but when referring to the children of serfs, they used the Latin word *sequelae* (litter). The word *sequelae* was used then, as it is now, to refer also to the progeny of dogs, cats, pigs, and other lesser animals. The gentry distinguished without hesitation between their own *liberi* and the serfs' *sequelae* because they knew that their children were superior and were entitled by natural right to be nonpoor, whereas the serfs were inferior and, in justice, poor. In medieval times, 99% of the population was poor. The 1% that was not poor presumed—without any doubts—that the descendants of the 99% would be poor forever.

The passing centuries brought persistent declines in the portion of the population living in poverty, and God continued to receive the blame—and the credit—for what was, at least by implication, a divinely ordained irreducible minimum of poverty in the world:

> God could have made all rich, or all men poor;
> But why He did not, let me tell wherefore:
> Had all been rich, where then had Patience been?
> Had all been poor, who had his Bounty seen?
> *Robert Herrick*[1]

By the nineteenth century, only 65 to 75% of the English and American populations were poor. But there were still some peo-

---

[1] "Riches and Poverty," *Poetical Works,* Oxford, 1915.

ple among the remaining 30% nonpoor who were convinced that the 65 to 75% were poor by irremedial heredity and that they would leave children equally poor. Mournful descriptions of the English poor included inspired prose; for example, these are the "dirtiest, laziest, most debased" people. A bleak future was forecast for them and their descendants. By the end of the nineteenth century, similar strictures were being applied to the urban poor of the industrializing America.

In the beginning of the present century, concern mounted in the United States regarding the "changeless race" of citizens whose progeny would be forever poor. This concern culminated in national opposition to the influx of new immigrants the people coming not from northwestern but from southern and eastern Europe: the Greeks, Italians, Spanish, Hungarians, Russians, and other Slavs. In 1920, the chief investigator for the House Committee on Immigration spoke for the native-born group when he summarized the findings of his study of the new immigrants:

The outstanding conclusion is that, making all logical allowances for environmental conditions, which may be unfavorable to the immigrant, the recent immigrants as a whole, present a higher percentage of inborn socially inadequate qualities than do the older stocks.[2]

This conclusion that the new immigrants were unchangeably inferior followed by 60 years an earlier conclusion of the contemporary native-born people that the Germans and Irish were unchangeably inferior. It also led to the expectation that the economy must prepare either to live with a growing number of doomed poor and their children or to exclude the new immigrants. The result was the enactment of legislation to exclude these immigrants. But the Greeks, Italians, and Slavs already here (like the Irish and Germans before them) moved gradually out of poverty and became attorneys, governors, CPA's, doctors, and bank presidents; and the percentage of the new immigrants living in poverty, like the percentage of old immigrants living in poverty, continued to decline with each decade.

---

[2] Cited by Oscar Handlin, *Race and Nationality in American Life*, Doubleday Anchor, Boston, 1957, p. 105.

In summary, the poor have always constituted a large portion of the population. Throughout history, commentators have observed the impoverished segment of the population and have speculated on why these people are poor. Over the years, the percentage of poor in the population has changed. Surveying the speculations and changes, the following things become apparent.

1. In every period of time, some commentators have asserted that a portion of their era's population was poor because it was the *nature* of these particular people (the serfs, laborers, the Germans, the Poles, or the Negroes) to be poor, and to remain poor along with their children, grandchildren, and great-grandchildren.

2. In Europe, before 1776, each century brought about a decrease in the portion of the population living in poverty. In the United States, after 1776, each decade did the same thing. Descendants of poor serfs, laborers, Germans, Poles, and Negroes became American executives.

3. Since the poor have declined in relative numbers, either the "naturally" unfit have become fit or each generation of poor has contained many persons with the potential, within themselves or within their children, to become nonpoor.

Examining the present situation, and looking into the future, we must wonder. Are most of today's poor impoverished because nature has equipped them only for poverty, so that they, their children, and their children's children must remain poor forever? Are the poor of the 1960's "one changeless race?" Or is there to be a continuing decline in the portion of the population who are poor?

I. DECLINE IN THE PERCENTAGE WHO ARE POOR

How much is known about the rate of decline in the percentage of the poor? Accounts from earlier periods in history suggest that 200 years ago most Americans were poor, that 50 years later the portion of poor had declined, and that successive decades had brought further improvement. Occasional statistics and many subjective observations support the generalization that the decline has been persistent, but before 1929 there was no single, consistent measure of the decline. Approximate statistics have been compiled for 1929 to 1948 to estimate the trend in the percentage of poor. Since 1948, this trend has been accurately measured.

The statistics were obtained from the annual incomes of families and of unattached individuals. But difficulties arise because of the price changes occurring during the years for which income statistics were collected. In 1929, incomes were spent in a market where consumer prices were 32% higher than prices in 1932. In 1932, incomes were spent in a market where consumer prices were only 43% of those of 1965. Since 1929, prices have changed each year from the levels of the preceding year. Comparison between the incomes of any two years within that period requires an appropriate allowance for price differences. These barriers can be overcome and allowances can be made.

A particular year must be selected as the base year, for example, 1954. Next, a typical family's selection of goods and services for that year must be identified: for example, 120 loaves of white bread, 31½ loaves of cracked wheat, 1⅜ loaves of rye bread, 117¼ pounds of potatoes, 89 pounds of hamburger, 1⅜ pairs of men's shoes, 1/8 of davenport, 1/16 of an appendectomy, 118 haircuts, 1/5 of a new car, and so on. Let us assume that an enormous supermarket cart is filled with these items (including the haircuts!), and that it is wheeled through the checkout counter. The clerk tallies the total cost of everything in the cart at 1954 prices. Then he adds up the bill again, using 1953 prices. The 1953 price total is compared to the 1954 total, showing that prices were 0.43% lower in 1953 than in 1954. The items are now tallied a third time and the amount is rung up using the prices of some other year—1929, for example—when prices were 36.22% lower than in 1954. The operation can be repeated for every year for which prices are available.

This process yields figures showing the percentage difference between consumer prices in the base year and in every other year under consideration. Then, incomes earned in different years can be compared by adjusting them to match the prices of the base year. For example, a family income of $637.80 spent in 1929 would have to be boosted to an even $1000 to buy the same amount in 1954.

After adjusting family and individual incomes of other years to the price levels prevailing in 1954, the U. S. Department of Commerce obtained the figures given in Table 4-1. These figures show for selected years the percentage of families and unattached individuals with annual incomes below $3000 and the percentage with annual incomes below $2000—with income figures adjusted to match 1954 prices. These statistics, freed from the influence of price changes, indicate that the decline in American poverty, no matter how it may be defined, has been persistent if not uniform during the period from 1929 to 1962.

The Census Bureau has not published statistics for the series shown in Table 4-1 for the years after 1962. Another series (Figure 4-1) may be better than that in Table 4-1 because it excludes unattached individuals. However, the series in Table 4-1 is shown first because it includes statistics for the 33-year period (1929 to 1962), whereas the series in Figure 4-1 does not begin until 1947.

Figure 4-1 uses family-income figures adjusted to the prices of 1964. These figures indicate declines, continuing through 1964, in both the *incidence* of poverty (using the simple $2999 criterion) and in the *number* of poor families. Will these declines continue? In the long run, they certainly will. For the short run, the answer is not so easy.

II. POVERTY AND ECONOMIC FLUCTUATIONS

Over the short run, the number of poor Americans varies with economic fluctuations. A way of showing the impact of economic fluctuations upon the number of poor Americans is the following one.

". . . to divide the fifteen years 1948–1963 into categories of strong economic expansion (1950, 1951, 1953, 1955, 1959, and 1962), slow expansion (1952, 1956, 1960, and 1963), and no expansion (1949, 1954, 1957, 1958, and 1961), and then to note what happened to the amount of poverty during each group of years. If the $3000 family-income measure is used, the results show that in years of strong expansion, the number of poor families declined by an average of 667,000 per year; in the slow-expansion years the decline was a

Table 4-1 Percent of Families and Unattached Individuals with Annual Income below $3000 and below $2000: All Figures Adjusted to 1954 Prices, Selected Years 1929 to 1962

Low-Income Category	Year										
	1929	1935 to 1936	1941	1944	1947	1950	1953	1956	1959	1962	
Percent under $2000	35.8	42.2	30.8	17.4	19.3	19.8	16.6	15.0	15.1	13.9	
Percent under $3000	59.2	62.6	47.1	31.6	34.9	34.5	29.0	25.6	25.9	23.9	

Source. U.S. Bureau of the Census, *Historical Statistics of the United States: Continuation to 1962 and Revisions,* U.S. Government Printing Office, Washington, D.C. 1965, pp. 23 and 114–115.

third less: 425,000 families per year; and in the no-expansion years of downturn or recession, the number of poor families *rose* by 400,000 per year. Thus, the difference between strong expansion and recession has been more than a million families (from a decrease of 667,000 to an increase of 400,000) among the poor." [3]

The bottom line in Figure 4-1 shows the number of families with an income below $3000. Small bumps in the line show the effects of economic fluctuations upon the number of poor families. In each of the recession years (1949, 1954, 1958, and 1961) the number of poor families increased, while during the years of recovery and expansion this number declined.

Table 4-2 shows the effects on the number of poor and on the incidence of poverty of the recession beginning in 1960 and of the record-breaking expansion that began in the spring of 1961. Based on the SSA criteria, these figures show growth in both the incidence of poverty and the number of poor Americans in 1960. Over the years since 1960, the figures show persistent declines in both the incidence of poverty and the number of poor Americans. This relationship between economic fluctuations and number of poor will be recalled later on, when we discuss the factors influencing economic fluctuations.

Table 4-2 Number and Percent of Poor in the Noninstitutional Population According to SSA Criteria for 1959 to 1964

| | Total Number of Persons (in Millions) | Poor[a] | |
| | | Number (in Millions) | Percent |
Year			
1959	176.5	38.9	22.1
1960	179.5	40.1	22.3
1961	181.4	38.1	21.1
1962	184.4	37.0	20.1
1963	187.2	35.3	18.9
1964	189.2	34.1	18.0

[a] In this SSA count, the poverty criteria for farm households were 70% (*not* 60%) of the poverty criteria for nonfarm households.

Source. Mollie Orshansky, "Recounting the Poor—A Five-Year Review," *Social Security Bulletin,* Vol. 29, No. 4, April 1966, p. 25.

[3] Burton A. Weisbrod (ed.), *The Economics of Poverty,* Prentice-Hall, Englewood Cliffs, N.J., 1965, pp. 15–16.

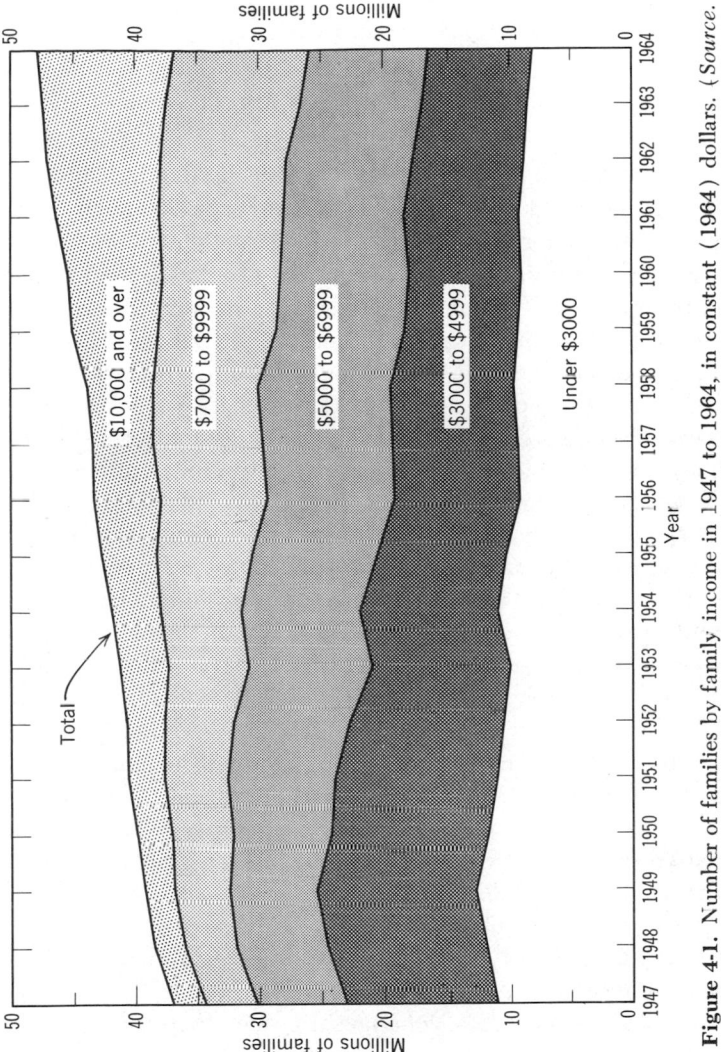

Figure 4-1. Number of families by family income in 1947 to 1964, in constant (1964) dollars. (*Source.* U.S. Bureau of the Census, *Current Population Reports*, Series P-60, No. 47, September 24, 1965, U.S. Government Printing Office, p. 1.)

III. POOR AND NONPOOR: VILLAGE
NEIGHBORS, CITY STRANGERS

As long as the frontier lasted in America, the poor and dissatisfied, the adventuresome and physically strong could move to fresh, new land. Enjoying the satisfactions of land ownership they could, in the short run, obtain a minimal amount of food, clothing, and shelter from their land while anticipating a far greater yield in the future. These adventurers thrust the frontier across the breadth of the continent, so that by 1890 the frontier was gone. Population movements thereafter were from farm to city, and the poor became increasingly urban with little or no land of their own and no way to obtain it.

Access to extensive land ownership, with its uncertain potential, may have been a great comfort to many nineteenth-century poor. But the closing of the frontier narrowed the range of opportunities for the twentieth-century poor and sent them to cities where few owned land and where the relationship between the poor and nonpoor was markedly different from their relationship when they lived together in small towns and rural townships. Before massive urbanizations, every rural township had both poor and nonpoor families, as did every small town. In these small towns and rural townships, each family knew every other family in the vicinity. Although a minority of Americans live this way today, it was not so long ago when a majority of them lived in rural areas. As late as 1900, the rural population of the United States was 50% greater than the urban population, and much of the population classified as "urban" in 1900 lived in towns of 2500 to 7500 people. Large cities were then exceptional. The typical living arrangements in the United States were those of Thornton Wilder's *Our Town*.

After 1900, technological changes in manufacturing and in agriculture accelerated rural outmigration. The nonfarm population grew rapidly while the farm population decreased in absolute as well as in relative numbers (the rural nonfarm population grew) during every decade after 1910. By 1920, the rural farm *and* rural nonfarm population was only 2% greater than the urban population; and by 1960, the urban population was 131% greater than the rural farm and rural nonfarm population.

In the small towns and rural townships, the farms or lots of the poor adjoined those of the nonpoor; the children of both played together. In emergencies involving fire or sickness, often in the face of death, they joined together to work, pray, and give comfort. The same was true in the case of gathering seasonal crops. Knowing the poor, the nonpoor extended charity. This charity was on a family-to-family basis or, at its remotest, on a church-to-family basis. In these townships and "Our Towns," the nonpoor knew of the problems of the poor as the problems of their neighbors.

In the sixties, the "Our Towns" have been superseded. The Chicago, Cincinnati, Nashville, and Seattle metropolitan areas have become the typical residential environments of the United States. No longer do poor and nonpoor live as neighbors. This is partly because the poor are relatively fewer in number than before, but mostly because each metropolitan area is divided into residential sections by income group. Formerly, small towns had right and wrong sides of the tracks, but the best and worst sections consisted of only a few blocks so that each touched directly upon blocks with families in quite different income groups. In the metropolitan areas of the 1960's, the best and the worst sections are so big that most of the residents in each area come into conversational contact only with people in income brackets near their own.

This arrangement keeps most of the nonpoor from knowing the poor. Perhaps most important, this isolation keeps most poor children from observing the behavior of the nonpoor, especially the behavior of nonpoor fathers. In small towns, the youthful poor know both the town's leading citizens and their children. Metropolitan areas isolate poor youth and leave them to learn of nonpoor adult behavior—if they learn at all—from books, movies, or TV.

Individual freedom depends, in large part, upon the ability of men and women to command goods and services. Poor people have restricted freedom. In the medieval period, when most people were poor, the freedom of choice for nearly everyone was narrowly restricted. In nineteenth-century America, when more than one half of the population lived in poverty, the freedom of choice for the majority remained limited, although the frontier offered alternative opportunities for some people. Throughout the present century, the persistent drop in the incidence of poverty has provided an ever-increasing segment of the population with a constantly expanding range of choice in ideas, movement, occupation, and consumption. As the decline in the number of poor Americans continues, the percentage of Americans having a widening range of choice will keep on rising.

IV. SUMMARY

Despite a frequently voiced assumption that the poor of the day represent a "changeless race"—an irreducible minimum—over the years there has been a persistent decline in the percentage of poor in the American population. This decline may continue, since the people who are poor in any particular year (whether German, Irish, Italian, Negro, or Puerto Rican) are not all poor because of inflexible laws of nature.

Over the long run, the incidence of poverty in the total population declines steadily. Over the short run, the number of poor families varies with economic fluctuations. During slack years, the number of poor families increases and during years of economic expansion this number falls, but the fall is more rapid during years of strong economic expansion than of weak economic expansion.

Despite the long-run decline in the incidence of poverty, millions of Americans remain poor, and their poverty is like that of the past in that their resources are slender compared to their needs. But the position of the poor in the 1960's is unlike the position of the poor in the past because most of today's poor live in isolated sections of cities cut off from the example of the nonpoor, while many nonpoor know of poverty only as a problem afflicting strangers.

Compared with the past, only a tiny portion of the American population is poor this year. Why has the incidence of poverty declined so steadily over the years? Why, despite the decline, are some people still poor while most Americans are not? The next four chapters explore the answers to these questions.

PART III

POVERTY: WHY DOES IT EXIST?

5

The Pie We Share

"Over the river and through the woods to grandmother's house we go," for Thanksgiving dinner. Among the good things on grandmother's table is a large pie. But no matter how big the pie is, if there are too many uncles, aunts, and cousins, the complaint will still be voiced, perhaps in a whisper, "Ma, there wasn't enough pie; I wish I could have had more."

We can think of America's total output as a pie—the pie of this year. Fancier than apple, mince, or even banana cream, this pie contains everything produced in the United States this year. It includes shoes, ships, sealing wax, cabbages (no kings), haircuts, bus rides, concerts, dog catchers' services, TV sets, police protection, and all of the other goods and services produced by Americans. This collection of goods and of services is called, appropriately, the national product.

If we continue to think of the national product as a huge pie, further analogy with the Thanksgiving pie is useful. The Thanksgiving pie pleases the taste and the stomach; the national product contains all the goods and services produced to please the whole range of American tastes. As with the Thanksgiving pie, the national product may be divided in a manner that leaves some people disgruntled over the size of their share.

The national product in the United States is precisely measured annually and even quarterly and monthly. This measurement provides accurate information regarding year-to-year changes in both total product and the amount per person. This chapter surveys the factors that determine the *total* size of the product and the per capita average; the following three chapters analyze the forces determining the *share* received by each individual in the nation. Together, these considerations explain why poverty exists.

I. GROWTH OF TOTAL PRODUCT VERSUS GROWTH OF PER CAPITA SHARE

Over time, growth in the size of the national product may yield each citizen a larger share. But if population grows faster than the national product, a drop in the share per person will follow. Insofar as per capita share is concerned, it is not the growth of total output that counts, but the growth of output relative to the growth of population.

The mythical Republic of Fertilvania provides an excellent example. The size of its national product increased 10% between 1956 and 1966 but, over the same period, its population increased 20%. Consequently, the size of the shares of national output available to individual residents decreased more than 8% during the decade.

If a nation's output is small, relative to its population, as it was in the Dominican Republic, India, and Egypt in 1965, then an equal division of this product will leave every citizen poor. Suppose a country's total output for one year is worth $40 billion; its population is 100 thousand; and the poverty line for the nation is $600 per person. Suppose initially, that income inequalities were great. Some people were very rich, and some were very poor. One thousand people averaged an income of $10,300 a year—a total of $10.3 million. The other 99 thousand people averaged an income of $300 a year—a total of $29.7 million. The income of each of the one thousand people was well above the $600 poverty line; the income of each of the 99 thousand was well below the $600 poverty line.

Then a revolution occurred and, in the year following the revolution, both the population and the national product were exactly the same size as before. Following the revolution, however, income inequality was abolished, and the national output was equally distributed among the nation's citizens. Every person then received an annual income of $400, just two thirds of the poverty-line figure. Everyone was poor.

In such a situation the only way poverty can be eliminated is by an increase in the size of the national product. The elimination of income inequality will make the poor less poor (in this country, $100 less poor), but poverty will not, indeed cannot, be eliminated.

Here the choice is between universal poverty and an arrangement in which a few can be rich and the many are each a little poorer than under a system of income equality. Until late in the nineteenth century, this was the condition of all mankind. The Golden Age of Greece was built on an unequal income distribution and left most Athenians in poverty while providing a fraction of them with comfortable incomes and time for the conceptual work that contributed so richly to the ideas and ideals of Western civilization. The splendors of the Roman Empire required great income inequalities. So did that "fleeting wisp of glory . . . that was known as Camelot." If all had been equal, *all* would have been poor.

In the nineteenth century, Karl Marx protested what he called the "exploitation" of the working class. Even then, the hard fact was that national products were still so small that an equal division of Germany's national product or an equal division of England's national product would have left everyone poor. If "exploited" at all, the workers were perhaps exploited by the low productivity of the time.

In classical Greece, in Arthur's England, and even in Victoria's England, there could be no end to poverty. There was simply not enough product to go around. Today, in Egypt, in India, and in the Dominican Republic there can be no end to poverty, at least not in the short run. There can be no end to poverty unless the national product rises relative to the national populations.

If a nation's product is large relative to its population, as in the United States, then an equal division of the output will leave *no* one poor. (An equal division might cause some men to work less hard, thereby reducing the total product, a phenomenon that is touched upon in the next chapter.) Given high output per person, a nation eliminating poverty through income transfers from its well-to-do to its poor can still retain wide income

differences among its citizens. For example, the United States
(as Chapter 3 pointed out) would have had no poverty in 1963
if $11.5 billion (1.9% of gross national product) had been trans-
ferred from the well-to-do to the people labeled poor by SSA
criteria. If such a transfer had been made, the differences in
income between the newly nonpoor and the well-to-do would
have remained large. This can happen only when a nation's per
capita product is high.

Now we turn to the processes that determine the size of the
national product relative to the size of the population. We draw
a distinction between the short run (in which the size and character of a nation's population and the size and character of a
nation's buildings and machinery do not change) and the long
run (in which the size and character of a nation's population,
buildings, and machinery can change). First, let us consider
the variables determining the size of national product in the
short run.

II. WHAT DETERMINES THE SIZE OF THE
NATIONAL PRODUCT IN THE SHORT RUN?

A. Natural Resources

Mauritania occupies 419,000 square miles of Africa's Atlantic
coast. Mauritania is the size of Texas and Montana combined.
It is big, but little fresh water touches the land, and few economically useful mineral concentrations have been found be-
neath the surface. Deficient in natural resources, the land re-
luctantly yields a very small output.

In contrast, Holland is only 4% as large as Mauritania. But the
ground is marvelously fertile, and rain is abundant; so the land
is a uniform luxuriant green, and the Dutch product is large.

Kuwait, which is a desert kingdom at the northern end of the
Persian Gulf and is only a little larger than the state of Connecticut, ranks fourth among the nations of the world in both
reserves and production of petroleum. In Kuwait, subsurface
wealth yields a rich black prize.

The character of a nation's natural resources—barren or fertile, wet or dry, impoverished or oiled—affects the size of the
output that the nation can produce.

B. Access to Transportation

In the interim between the two world wars, the world smiled because the dictator of Hungary bore the title Admiral, although Hungary was located 160 miles from the nearest salt water. Yet Hungary, astride the navigable Danube, was and is much more efficiently equipped for cheap transportation than mountainous Bolivia, Paraguay, Zambia, and Nepal, which have neither salt-water ports nor navigable rivers.

In order to produce a large output, there must be a moving around of people, raw materials, semifinished parts, and final products. The position of the land makes a big difference in the size of the natural product because producers deciding among locations will avoid areas where transportation is difficult; obviously, extra effort required to move things leaves less effort to make things.

C. The Quantity of Physical Capital

There are about 97 million Japanese living on the Japanese islands. Their per capita output is about one half of the output per American. If a playful god on Mt. Olympus were to grasp all 97 million Japanese, pick them up, and put them down in the United States in place of 97 million Americans transplanted to Japan, what would happen to total production in both countries? Would the output of the Japanese islands double to give the immigrant Americans the same per capita share that they enjoyed at home? Would American output sharply contract under half-Japanese operation?

To answer these questions, another one must be raised: How does the quantity of equipment used by the typical Japanese worker compare to the quantity of equipment used by the typical American worker? The answer is easy. The typical American worker uses much more equipment than his Japanese counterpart. More machinery means more product per worker. Much of the Japanese-American difference in per capita product is due to the difference between the two countries in the amount of tools, buildings, and machinery—technically called physical capital—per worker.

The population exchange between Japan and the United

States would leave the Americans in Japan with a small amount of physical capital per worker and would give the Japanese in America about twice as much physical capital per worker as they had in Japan. After the exchange, time would be required to change the language of the safety warnings and permit workers to adjust to unfamiliar equipment. Following this transition period, the output produced by Americans on the Japanese islands would be about the same as had formerly been produced by the Japanese. The size of the American output would be about the same under 50% Japanese hands and 50% American hands as it would be if all of the output were produced by American hands. American workers in Japan would produce only one half as much per worker as they had produced at home. Japanese in the United States would produce about twice as much per worker as they had produced in Japan. The amount of total and per capita output produced in a nation depends, in large part, on the quantity of physical capital per worker.

D. The Quantity of Human Capital

As a variation upon the previous population switch, suppose the god on Mt. Olympus traded the entire American population for a population of equal size, age, and sex from the subcontinent of India. What would the Indians be able to do in the United States with their sudden wealth of machinery?

Among the Japanese population, 98% are literate. Among the United States population, 97% are literate. Among the Indian population, 18% are literate. Because of these differences in literacy and because of differences between India and Japan in experience with machinery, the question, "What could the Indians do with American machinery?" is answered differently from the question, "What could the Japanese do with American machinery?" For the Indians, the question can be reworded to ask, "What use could be made of America's physical capital by a largely illiterate population inexperienced in the use of nuts, bolts, and lubricants, much less in pistons, transistors, and IBM cards?" Clearly, the answer is, "Very little."

It is not enough to *possess* a tractor, a lathe, or a computer, that is to say, it is not enough to *have* physical capital. Workers must also know *how to use* the machinery. Knowing how to use a particular piece of equipment involves even more than knowing only the mechanics of the unit. The effective operator must be able to coordinate with other machines, other operators, and managers. The operator must be able to deal with the expected contingencies by following directions. He must know enough about mechanical relationships to be able to deal with the unexpected things to prevent damage to his machine. In a general sense, much of this means that he must think habitually in terms of sequential cause and effect, that is to say, he must think rationally.

Reading, writing, arithmetic, rationality, and all other productive skills are *human* capital. Human capital derives from parental instruction, formal education, on-the-job training, and years of experience. The size of a nation's product is as directly dependent upon its accumulation of human capital as upon its accumulation of physical capital. America's per capita national product exceeds Japan's because America has nearly double the per capita physical capital of Japan and exceeds India's because America has far more physical capital and far more human capital per person. The United States per capita national product in the 1960's is much greater than it was in the nineteenth century because the United States now has far more physical and human capital per person that at any time in the nineteenth century.

E. Technological Quality

Some lathes are better than other lathes; some student engineers are taught engineering techniques that are superior to those taught other student engineers. The national product derives from an accumulation of physical and human capital whose potential is a function of both quantity *and* quality. The higher the quality of a nation's physical and human capital (in other words, the better its technology), the larger is the potential national product.

F. Hours Worked per Year

In the nineteenth century, most Americans worked 60, 70, or more hours a week; vacations were infrequent and brief. Since 1900, the length of the average work week has gradually fallen from 55 to 48 to 44 to 40 hours; the number and length of vacations have grown. Since the Civil War, hours worked per year have fallen about 40% for the average worker. In other countries today, most people work far more hours per year than Americans. Given the amount of capital per worker, it is clear that the more hours worked by a nation's labor force, the greater will be the total and the per capita national product, and vice versa.

G. Size of Population

The size of a country's product is also affected by the size of its population. As a rule of thumb, the larger a nation's population, the larger is its labor force; and the larger a nation's labor force, the larger is its output. But large population, although assuring a large total product, may (as in India today), result in a small share for each person. Population size, possessed of the power both to loosen total production and bind per capita income, occupies a unique resource position that requires special attention in subsequent pages.

H. Aggregate Demand

In 1932, the idle ships and freight cars, the silent, padlocked mines, the oiled but inactive cranes, and the motionless assembly lines were American physical capital in disuse. The unemployed patternmakers, the former personnel managers selling apples, the skilled brick masons employed as common laborers were unused American human capital.

Mark Twain once observed that those who could read but did not were no better off than those who could not read. Similarly, a nation that has resources but does not use them is no better off than the nation without them. Land, buildings, equipment, education, and training are productive only if they are used, and they are used only if there is an effective demand for their use. The relevant phrase is "aggregate demand"—the demand from all businesses, all governments, and all households. If aggregate demand is "sufficient," then all the available resources will be used, and the national product will, assuming no special distortions, be maximized. If aggregate demand is insufficient, then some resources will stand idle. If aggregate demand is excessive, all resources will be used *and* prices will be forced up. This point is discussed further at the end of this chapter.

III. WHAT DETERMINES THE SIZE OF THE PRODUCT IN THE LONG RUN?

The preceding comment refers to the short run, the period in which the character of technical knowledge, the number of workers, and the quantities of human and physical capital are fixed. The potential size of the national product is then limited by fixed quantities of knowledge and resources. The actual size of the product is determined in the short run by these factors and by aggregate demand.

In time, these factors change. In the long run, the size of the product may grow or shrink as the quality of knowledge and the quantity and quality of resources rise or fall and aggregate demand fluctuates.

A. Growth in Physical Capital

National product can be measured two ways: net or gross. The difference between net and gross is equal to the amount of a nation's physical capital used up during a period of production. In 1965, the United States contained about $1.2 trillion worth of business inventories, of residential, government, institutional, and business structures, and of producers' durable equipment (for example, assembly lines, lathes, blast furnaces). This was the physical capital used to produce the national product of 1965. In producing the year's national product, this physical capital suffered extensive depreciation as the wear and tear of use wore it down; some of it was destroyed by fire or other accident.

Gross national product is the total new output of a year. *Net national product* is that total less an amount exactly offsetting the physical capital worn out, burned, or otherwise destroyed during the year. In other words, net national product is total production above and beyond that required to hold constant the nation's stock of structures, business inventories, and producers' equipment. The earlier sections of this chapter have used the abbreviated term national product for the actual term *net national product.*

Annual gross national product is always divided in two parts: one part offsets physical capital used up during the year; the other part is net national product. The net national product is, in turn, divided into two parts: one part is itself used up—consumed—during the year; the other part is added in structures, inventories, and producers' durable equipment to the physical capital that will help produce the next year's output. The addition to physical capital is called *net investment.* Each year's division of net national product as between consumption and net investment has important implications for the potential net national product of later years.

Japan provides one kind of extreme example. The Japanese gross national product, like that of all nations, is divided into three parts. In recent years 9% has been used to offset accidental losses and depreciation caused by the year's production. The largest share, 63%, has been consumed in the year of production. The third share (a large share by international standards) 28% of gross national product, has been used to add to the stock of physical capital.

Because of this willingness and ability to hold consumption and depreciation well below total output, Japan's stock of physical capital has grown substantially from year to year. Because of the growth in the stock of Japanese capital, the *potential* size of the Japanese net national product has grown substantially year after year; and because aggregate demand has grown proportionately, the *actual* size of the Japanese per capita share has grown 9.1% a year, a rate of growth well above that of any other nation.

As a contrasting example, we may imagine conditions in England during a medieval decade in which neither war nor technological change touched the land. In the first year of the decade, production might have been divided into two parts, the lesser part being used to offset the year's depreciation in buildings and tools, the greater part going to current consumption (mostly food). During the second year of the decade, the national output might have been similarly divided. If, in every year of the decade, production was entirely used up in depreciation and current consumption, then, assuming no change in population, the size of England's output would have been exactly the same in the last as in the first year of the decade.

There was no change because, by the assumptions made, there was no net investment during the decade. In every nation in every year a large or a small portion of the national product may be used to add to physical capital. The larger the portion devoted to such additions, the larger will be the year-to-year growth in a nation's potential total output. The smaller the portion of the product used to increase physical capital, the smaller will be the year-to-year growth.

B. Growth in Human Capital

All that has been said of the effects of net investment in physical capital applies equally to net additions to human capital. The United States Department of Commerce estimates the size of each year's addition to physical capital, but not the size of each year's addition to human capital. Changes in human capital, although unmeasured, do occur, and when they do, the potential total national product increases.

C. Technological Change

When one lathe is replaced by two lathes exactly like the original one, the change that takes place is neither invention nor innovation. But when a lathe that is superior to the original one is conceived and built for tests, invention occurs. When the superior lathe replaces the original lathe, the change is properly called innovation.

Invention is the conception, construction, and use of new machines and techniques in a laboratory or testing facility. Innovation is the application of the new machine or technique to production. The discovery and application of ever-superior technology is a major source of year-to-year increases in the American national product. In every land and climate, innovation can serve to increase both total and per capita output.[1]

---

[1] For a more complete analysis of the means and the obstacles to economic development in countries like India, see Robert Baldwin, *Economic Development and Growth,* in this series.

D. Growth in Population

In general, the more rapidly the population grows, the more rapidly the labor force grows; and the more rapidly the labor force grows, the more rapidly the national output grows. However, in the long run as in the short run, the role of population remains ambiguous in its effect upon per capita share. Circumstances sometimes exist in which population growth is associated with growth of total product and decline in per capita portion. This is the case whenever percentage growth in population exceeds percentage growth in output.

E. Aggregate Demand

Growth in the quantity and quality of national resources increases the *potential* size of a nation's product. The actual *size* at any time may be less than the potential. As in both the short and long run, aggregate demand must be sufficient to bring about total utilization of a nation's resources if the national product is to be maximized. As a nation's population, technical know-how, and physical and human capital increase over time, the nation's aggregate demand must increase proportionately or a rising share of available resources will stand idle.

IV. POTENTIAL OUTPUT AND ACTUAL OUTPUT

Aggregate demand determines the size of the difference between potential and actual net national product (NNP). Aggregate demand is sufficient when actual NNP about equals the NNP possible with existing resources during a particular time period. How can the term "sufficient" be measured statistically? What forces determine the strength of aggregate demand?

Sufficient demand means that all available resources are being employed. There is work for all who want to work. In the United States, statistics are collected monthly to measure employment rates. These rates show the extent to which human resources are being used. Since mobility between jobs involves lags in locating work and getting started, since some of the unemployed have little ability, and since some people want work, but not very badly, full employment of "all who want work" leaves 3 to 4% of the American labor force unemployed in the statistical count. Thus, demand is sufficient when unemployment equals about 3½% of the labor force. Demand is deficient—in the sense used here—when unemployment moves up toward 4%. Demand is excessive when employers press unemployment below 3½% and prices rise rapidly. (Chapter 11 notes that prices rise in the United States at unemployment levels above 3½%.)

In order to survey the forces affecting the strength of aggregate demand, it is helpful to separate NNP into three components by distinguishing among goods and services used for current consumption, for net investment, and for public (government) use. This breakdown may be written as:

$$\text{aggregate demand} = \text{actual } NNP = C + I + G$$

A great many factors act together to determine the amounts that households, businesses, and governments are able and willing to buy. Household and business demands are influenced by current levels of employment, income, prices, and profits, and by expectations regarding future levels of employment, income, prices, and profits. Inventions, politics, war, and rumors of wars play a part along with all future expectations. State and local taxes affect private demands. Government demand fluctuates with the decisions of Congress, state legislatures, city councils, school boards, and public tax referenda.

Two factors acting on aggregate demand require special attention. These are the fiscal and monetary policies of the Federal Government. The Government has discretion to vary these policies and can use them to prod actual NNP in the direction of potential NNP.[2]

Monetary policy is particularly important because of the constraint acting perpetually upon aggregate demand and represented by the formula:

$$\text{aggregate demand} = NNP = MV = PT$$

The meaning of the letters in the formula can be illustrated with 1965 statistics. In 1965, net national product was about $616 billion. M is the amount of money in the country; in 1965, it was something over $154 billion. The individual dollars of a $154 billion money supply would have had to change hands

---

[2] For a more extensive analysis of the relationships among monetary and fiscal policy, other variables, and aggregate demand, see Arnold Collery, *National Income and Employment Analysis,* in this series.

an average of four times that year to pay for the $616 billion net national product (*V* represents that four times).

T is the sum of what businesses, governments, and households buy; it is the total number of final sales in a year of ice cream cones, haircuts, cars, airplane rides, new homes, television repairs, locomotives, lathes, rockets, and so on. *P* is the average price of all those sales. If in 1965, there were 308 billion final sales (the actual number is unknown and unneeded), then *P* was $2.

The relationship $MV = PT$ is a truism, applicable to all times and in all places using money; but it is a useful truism. In this equation, *T* represents the nation's total net physical output, and *PT* represents the dollar value of that output.

Over time, the labor force and the quantity and quality of physical and human capital in the United States grow bigger. As these factors increase, there is an increase in the potential size of *T*. In the United States the size of *V* may be assumed to change little from year to year, and *P* rarely falls. If *V* and *P* hold roughly constant, then actual *T* can rise as much as potential *T* *only* if *M* rises.

If the United States, *M* is restricted by the discretionary activity of the Board of Governors of the Federal Reserve System. The Board can permit *M* to rise slowly or rapidly, it can hold *M* constant or force *M* down. But the Board is limited in its ability to force *M* up. Increases in *M* depend in the main upon increases in borrowing from private commercial banks. The Board can authorize increased borrowing, but it cannot force individuals or corporations to borrow. Even if the Board is successful in an attempt to raise *M*, *T* may be little affected if *V* falls or if *P* rises. Inability to translate monetary policy into higher *T* was evident in the United States during the 1930's—perhaps because monetary policy was "inept." [3] When monetary policy attempts to raise *T* and fails to raise it the desired amount, then fiscal policy can be used to push actual *T* near the level of potential *T*.

Fiscal policy refers to changes in the levels of *G* and of tax

---

[3] For an argument that monetary policy was inept, see Milton Friedman and Anna J. Schwartz, *The Great Contraction: 1929–1933*, Princeton University Press, Princeton, N. J., 1965.

collections. If the Federal Government raises G, then the G component of aggregate demand increases. If the Federal Government cuts taxes, households and businesses will have larger disposable incomes and may raise C and I (or may lend the extra income back to the Federal Government).

In the other direction, reduced Federal Government spending or higher taxes may press down on aggregate demand (emphasis is on federal rather than on state and local government spending and taxes because the Federal Government has more discretion in setting taxing and spending levels). But fiscal policy cannot achieve its objectives unless monetary policy helps. For example, if G rises while M, V, and P remain constant, T cannot rise and I and C, the private sector, must be cut back to offset the increase in G, the public sector of the economy. Conversely, higher taxes and lower G may not reduce T if monetary policy permits increases in I and in C which cause a net increase in T. Fiscal policy can be very effective in pushing actual T close to potential T (witness the effects of the 1964 and 1965 federal tax cuts), but only if monetary policy points in the same direction, as it did during the 1964 to 1965 period.

V. SUMMARY

People live in poverty when their essential needs exceed the goods and services available to them. Apart from goods employed to offset the physical capital used up, a nation's people cannot have any more goods and services in any year than they produce during that year (or import net of exports). A nation's total output is called *gross national product*. A nation's output, less the goods used to offset the physical capital used up during a year, is called *net national product*.

Per capita net national product depends on the size of the net national product relative to the size of the national population. The net national product of a nation may be so small relative to its population that an equal distribution of its output would leave all citizens poor. This was the cause of poverty throughout the world from primitive times until very recently. Even in nineteenth century England the working classes received low incomes because net national product was low. An equal division of output would have made the poor less poor but would have left everyone poor. All of the underdeveloped countries are in this position today. No amount of domestic altruism can wipe out poverty when net national product is less than the population size times the essential needs of the average citizen.

In contrast, in countries with net national product large relative to population size, poverty can be eliminated even though there remain wide inequalities in income distribution. The United States and most western European countries are now in this position.

In the short run, in a period so short that the relevant variables do not change, the size of the net national product depends on natural resources, geography, quantity and quality of physical and of human capital, average annual working hours, and aggregate demand. Per capita net national product depends on the fruits of these variables relative to population size. In the long run, changes in potential total and in potential per capita net national product depend on changes in each of these variables.

Aggregate demand determines the size of the difference between potential and actual net national product (NNP). Aggregate demand is sufficient when actual NNP is about equal to potential NNP. Unemployment statistics have been introduced as a measure of the sufficiency of aggregate demand in the United States. For the purposes of this book, sufficient aggregate demand has been defined as the situation in which the unemployment rate lies between 3 and 4%.

Aggregate demand is the sum of the separate demands of households, businesses, and governments for consumption, net investment, and public (government) goods and services. Thus, aggregate demand $= NNP = C + I + G$. A host of factors operate together to determine the amount that households, businesses, and governments are able and willing to buy. Two of these factors have received special attention here. These two have been the fiscal and monetary policies that the Federal Government is able to use to prod actual NNP in the direction of potential NNP.

Monetary policy is particularly important because of the constraint that aggregate demand $= NNP = MV = PT$ where M is the quantity of money, V the velocity of money, P is the average price, and T is the number of the units of goods and services produced net during a time period. Then T equals the nation's total net physical output, and PT equals the dollar value of the net output. In the United States each year, the labor force and the quantity and quality of physical and human capital increase permitting an increase in T. If V and P hold roughly constant, actual T can rise as much as potential T only if M rises.

The Federal Reserve Banks bear the responsibility for United States monetary policy. Striving for sufficient demand *and* stable price levels, the Federal Reserve can prevent increases in M and can even force it down. It can authorize increases in M but cannot always force M up. Sometimes when M rises, the Federal Reserve finds that falling V or rising P reduces the impact on T of the higher M. If monetary policy directed toward raising T falls, for one reason or another, fiscal policy can be used to raise aggregate demand and lift actual T to the potential permitted by the physical and human resources of the United States.

To raise T, fiscal policy can take the form of higher G, lower taxes to raise C and I, or both higher G and lower taxes. In any use of fiscal policy, monetary policy is of preeminent importance because, if V and P hold constant, T can rise, whether pushed up by C by I, or by G, *only* if the Federal Reserve permits M to rise.

Similarly, when an increase in taxes or a decrease in G is used to curb aggregate demand which would raise P excessively, the object is achieved only if monetary policy also acts to restrain MV. Together fiscal and monetary policy represent the principal tools used by the Federal Government to influence aggregate demand in order to restrain prices while pressing actual T to rise to the level of potential T.

This chapter has considered, first, the variety of factors determining the potential size of NNP and, second, monetary and fiscal policies influencing the actual size of NNP. The next three chapters examine the process that governs the distribution of the American NNP. The primary purpose is to analyze the parts of the process that leave some Americans poor.

6

Dividing the National Product

The amount of poverty in a nation depends, first, on the size of its gross national product and, second, on the way in which that product is distributed. In the United States, the gross national product (GNP) is large. In 1965, it was worth $675 billion in current prices. Table 6-1 shows GNP for 1929, for 1965, and for the election years between.

Table 6-1 Gross National Product in 1958 Dollars—Total and Per Capita; and United States Population in 1965, 1929, and in the Election Years, 1932 to 1964

Year	Gross National Product (Billions)	Population (Millions)	Per Capita Gross National Product
1929	$203.6	121.8	$1672
1932	144.1	124.8	1154
1936	193.0	128.1	1506
1940	227.2	132.1	1719
1944	361.3	138.4	2610
1948	323.6	146.6	2210
1952	392.1	156.9	2499
1956	446.1	168.2	2652
1960	487.8	180.7	2700
1964	577.6	192.1	3007
1965	609.0	194.6	3124

Source. Economic Report of the President: 1966, U. S. Government Printing Office, Washington, D.C., 1966, pp. 210 and 231.

If the actual dollar value of the 1932 GNP were compared with the dollar value of the 1965 GNP, the 1965 figure would be larger for two reasons: first, because more units were produced in 1965 and, second, because prices per unit were up 175% from 1932 to 1965. The statistics of Table 6-1 have been adjusted to show only changes in units; the effects of price changes have been eliminated. In substance, the 1932 product was loaded into an oversized supermarket cart and wheeled past the check-out clerk, who totaled up the value of the 1932 soup, cars, firemen, medical care, new roads, drill presses, houses, apples, dog-catchers, haircuts, and so on, in 1958 prices. The same procedure was followed for the total product of every other year in Table 6-1. With the impact of price changes removed, the GNP figures of Table 6-1 show real changes in output with *every* unit valued in 1958 prices (NNP would be used here, but there is no NNP series adjusted for price changes).

As Table 6-1 shows, there were exceptions to the rule that American output grows steadily larger. Between 1944 and 1948 and between 1929 and 1932, real GNP fell. Although not shown in Table 6-1, there were declines from the preceding year in 1933, 1938, 1954, and 1958. However, over most periods, GNP grows larger, trebling between 1929 and 1965.

With respect to poverty, total product is important, but per capita product is more important. As the mythical republic in Chapter 5 demonstrated (p. 48), a rise in total product need not result in increased product per person. If the percentage of population increase exceeds the percentage of increases in gross national product, per capita output will fall.

Table 6-1 shows that from 1929 to 1965 the population of the United States steadily increased. Yet, as the last column of the table indicates, the increase in population, although large, was never large enough in the years shown to offset the increase in GNP.

The principal point here is that every time per capita GNP rises, there is an increase in the *ability* of the United States to reduce poverty. But the whole GNP does not go to private persons. A large part of it goes to counties, school districts, cities, townships, and states. An almost equally large part goes to the Federal Government, most of this being used for national defense. (Over the period 1951 to 1964, more went to the federal than to state and local governments, but the lead passed from the Federal Government in 1965 as a result of persistent growth in the state and local governments' share while the Federal Government's share declined slightly.)

Table 6-2 shows how the national product is broken down between the public and private sectors of the economy. In 1965, 7.4% of the GNP went to national defense, another 2.5% to other federal uses, 10.1% to state and local governments, and 80.0% remained for the private sector.

When interpreting these figures, we must bear in mind that social security payments, veterans' pensions, aid to the blind, and other *transfers* from governments do *not* show up in the government columns of Table 6-2. This table shows neither total

Table 6-2 Division of the Gross National Product in 1965 and in the Election Years 1932 to 1964, by Percentage Shares

	Percent of National Product going to:				
	The Public Sector			The Private Sector	
	Federal				
Year	National Defense	Other	State and Local	Investment	Consumption
1932	2.5ᵃ		11.3	2.4	83.8
1936	6.0ᵃ		8.5	10.5	75.0
1940	2.2	3.8	8.1	14.9	71.0
1944	41.5	0.8	3.6	2.5	51.5
1948	4.2	2.3	5.8	20.3	67.4
1952	13.3	1.7	6.6	15.7	62.7
1956	9.6	1.3	7.9	17.7	63.5
1960	8.9	1.7	9.2	15.7	64.4
1964	7.9	2.5	10.0	16.2	63.4
1965	7.4	2.5	10.1	16.6	63.4

ᵃ These figures are for national defense and other federal uses combined.

Source. Calculated from the *Economic Report of the President: 1966*, U.S. Government Printing Office, Washington, D.C., 1966, p. 209.

tax collections nor the total of government checks written. It shows the division of real GNP between public and private uses. In this regard, Table 6-2 shows governments receiving 20.0% and the private sector 80.0% in 1965. The larger the portion going to government (21.6% in 1952, 45.9% in 1944), the less is available to the private sector; and the less available to the private sector, the more extensive poverty is likely to be. Since 1956 the government share has risen slightly, as the decline in the federal share has not quite offset the growth of the state and local government share.

The private share has remained about the same since 1956, but not all of the private share goes into consumption. Part of it goes to replace depreciation and part into new buildings, machinery, and business inventories; that is to say, part of the private share goes into gross investment.

Gross investment is larger than net investment—the concept introduced in the previous chapter. Gross investment is the sum of the buildings, equipment, and inventories produced during a year. Net investment is the *addition* to a nation's physical capital after compensating for all depreciation and other destruction of the capital stock with which the country began the year.

The problem of "more or less investment this year" is also a problem of "more or less poverty this year, less or more poverty in the future." The larger this year's consumption, the less there will be left over for investment and the less poverty there will be this year, but the lower the production and the greater the poverty in the future. Conversely, the smaller this year's consumption, the more there will be left over for investment and the greater will be the poverty this year, but the greater the production and the smaller the poverty in the future. The poverty of nineteenth-century England and America was greater than otherwise because a large share of nineteenth-century output went into net investment. The low incidence of poverty in the United States in the 1960's is the consequence of the high levels of net investment in the past.

The last two columns of Table 6-2 disclose the share of GNP going to private gross investment and the share to private consumption. In the past, these shares have fluctuated when de-

68   *Dividing the National Product*

pression or war disrupted the economy. Since the Korean War, the consumption share has remained almost constant while the investment share has varied only enough to cause mild business fluctuations.

Table 6-2 indicates the percentage of GNP going to various uses. Table 6-3 shows the per capita dollar output going to the private sector. The dollar figures of Table 6-3 are not the current dollars but have been adjusted to reflect 1958 prices.

Table 6-3 Per Capita Product Going into Private Hands, in 1965 and in the Election Years 1932 to 1964 (in 1958 Dollars)

	Per Capita Private Product		
Year	Total ($) (1)	Gross Investment ($) (2)	Consumption ($) (3)
1932	962	42	920
1936	1258	178	1080
1940	1444	265	1179
1944	1297	59	1238
1948	1892	454	1438
1952	1912	386	1526
1956	2145	472	1673
1960	2174	424	1750
1964	2430	493	1937
1965	2550	525	2025

Source. Calculated from the *Economic Report of the President: 1966*, U.S. Government Printing Office, Washington, D.C., 1966, p. 210.

The first column of Table 6-3 lists total per capita private product in 1965 and in each recent presidential election year; the second and third columns reflect the breakdown as between gross investment and consumption. Each figure in the first column shows the amount each person would obtain in a particular year if the product to which private individuals take title each year were distributed equally among all Americans. The amount is far above the poverty line and, except during the Second World War, has been rising persistently.

The second column of Table 6-3 presents the variability of per capita gross investment (again in 1958 dollar values). The third column reports per capita consumption, in 1958 dollars, for 1965 and for each recent presidential election year. This measure has increased persistently, more than doubling between 1932 and 1964. If all of the increase had gone to the nonpoor, the incidence of poverty might have held constant or risen. But, in the United States, this increase in per capita consumption was shared between poor and nonpoor and brought the decline in poverty described in Chapter 4.

I. DIVIDING THE PRIVATE SHARE

As the American national product is divided between governments and the private sector, and as the private sector's share is divided between investment and consumption, both the consumption and title to investment portions are distributed among the total population. No natural law exists to determine the character of this distribution. The method followed in the United States works in that its results are so generally accepted that only an infinitesimal number of Americans favor fundamental changes in the basic system. But there are other systems of distribution that could be used, some of which have been used at other times and in other places. Within the context of this book, the particular system used is important because, given the ratio of output to population, the particular method used determines the incidence of poverty in the economy. Three of these other systems are considered here: (1) perfect equality, (2) authority-tradition, and (3) to each according to his needs. After surveying these three systems, the remainder of the chapter concentrates upon the American system of distribution.

Let us first consider equality of income distribution. The concept of output per person has been frequently used in our previous discussion. For any given time and place, the dollar figure of output per person is the amount that each person would receive if net national product (NNP) were equally divided among the members of the population (alternatively gross national product could be used in this calculation but net output is more appropriate for long-run measures relevant to incidence of poverty). If America's 1965 NNP of

$616.8 billion had been divided equally among the 194.6 billion total population of the United States, each would have received $3170. If the private portion of the 1965 NNP, including net investment as well as consumption, had been divided equally among the 194.6 billion population, each would have received $2475. A couple living alone would have received $4950; a family of four would have received $9900.

It is easy to calculate the numerical outcome of equality of income distribution, but it is difficult to find examples. The mechanics required to bring about such a distribution are hard to imagine. The effects of this system upon total production are problematical, but total effort and total output is likely to be small when extra effort by an individual would have little impact on his income. Whatever the total output and whatever the mechanics that affect equality of income distribution, the system would be likely to encourage large families.

A second system of distribution is that of authoritarianism, generally tempered by tradition. This system has been widely used in the past and is being widely used this year. In the Western world, the most famous example is that which led to the quarrel around which *The Iliad* revolves. Included in the Greek national output of 1269 B.C., along with home-grown grapes, lambs, and olives, were the spoils of war. As part of their year's work, the Greeks sacked Thebe. Included in the booty were the two girls, Chryseis and Briseis. How was the Greek national product (including the girls and other items acquired in pillage) to be divided?

Agamemnon, as commander in chief, was invested with supreme authority. As Calcus, the seer, put it, "Agamemnon's authority is absolute among us"; his "word is law to all Greeks." However, this authority was tempered by tradition, and it was the troops who, exercising their traditional right, decided that Agamemnon's prize should be Chryseis because they thought that she was the most attractive woman among the captives. It was the soldiers again who awarded Briseis to Achilles after judging her the second most attractive prisoner. Yet when the god, Apollo, intervened to force Agamemnon to return Chryseis to her priest father, authority overrode tradition, and Agamemnon took Briseis away from Achilles causing that prince to sulk in his tent until the Trojans had mauled the Greeks so badly that Agamemnon was willing to return Briseis and apologize.

In most cases the man exercising authority has divided the national output in a way best calculated (in his opinion) to maximize his well-being; and, for him, a continued tenure in office has usually been a primary consideration. Tradition has operated to formalize the practices of dividing the product, which the authoritarian must observe unless he is willing to risk his office. Feudalism, slavery (with Germany and Russia providing recent vivid illustrations), prison labor, sharecropping in the American South, peonage, and the care of children by parents all involve mixtures of authoritarianism and tradition, and have played essential roles in dividing national products.

The third system is more talked about than acted upon. As Marx observed in 1875, "From each according to his abilities, to each according to his needs." This observation has long been famous as a third method of dividing the national product. Marx plagiarized freely from the anarchist Bakunin who, in 1870, published a declaration urging, "From each according to his faculties, to each according to his needs." Before Bakunin, collectivist and cooperative societies in Britain, France, and America had dedicated themselves to this program. The fundamental difficulty with the program is that needs are not measurable by objective standards that would permit individual comparisons of the intensity of personal needs. A group with Bakunin's objectives has no obvious criteria to guide it in dividing output. The group may agree on which needs will be satisfied first and second, but may disagree acrimoniously in trying to decide between the twelfth and thirteenth places.

To illustrate the point, suppose that 100 families had 10 million units of penicillin, 8 straight chairs, 2 stuffed chairs, 8 cotton suits, and 3 wool suits to be distributed in 1 year. Ideally, goods should be distributed according to needs so that the last unit of output to each person would satisfy exactly the same intensity of personal need. Who is to decide upon the intensity of each person's needs? A doctor could select the people to receive the penicillin, but what measures of need could be used to determine who should get the straight chairs, who the stuffed chairs, who the cotton suits, who the wool suits? As a practical matter, most nineteenth-century collectivist societies, which organized around this philosophy of distribution according to need, found it necessary to select a particular person to decide whose needs were greatest. At that point, the system became authoritarian, and volunteer members began to drop out. Twentieth-century communists frequently pay lip service to the Marxian principle but do *not* organize their economies to implement it.

If the United States were to convert peacefully to the authoritarian system of distribution, the effects on the incidence and character of poverty would be problematical. If the United States were peacefully converted to income equality or to distribution according to need, there would be *no* poverty in the United States—or, stated more cautiously, there would be no poverty if total output, which might fall, were to remain at least one half as great as it is now.

There is a fourth method by which the national product can be divided. This system follows the guiding rule, "to each according to his contribution to production." If this program is followed, then a totally disabled man will quickly die, and a Mr. X with twice the productivity of a Mr. Z will receive twice the share of national product as Mr. Z. Mr. Z may be diabetic, his wife may be bedridden, and Mr. X's family may be in excellent health; these differences in need have no impact upon the distribution of the national product.

The American system of private property and markets approximates the fourth pattern of rewards in proportion to contributions. A multitude of market imperfections results in some people receiving more than they contribute while others receive less. Some groups benefit from monopoly incomes. Private charity and the coercive authority of county, city, federal, and state governments take from some and give to others to meet needs deemed both acute and otherwise likely to be unmet. Yet the basic American rule and, incidentally, the basic Russian rule is to distribute the output in proportion to productive contribution.

Would some other system be better? The answer is a matter of opinion, but most Americans have concluded that the best system for distributing the private share of NNP resembles the one used in the United States in the 1960's.

II. THE DETERMINANTS OF PRODUCTIVE INTELLIGENCE

As long as the American system distributes output in approximate proportion to productive contribution, the productive contribution of individuals is of primary importance in determining who shall be poor and who shall be nonpoor. The determinants of an individual's potential productive contribution are of two kinds: the physical materials used by him in production, and his productive intelligence. The physical materials derive from the soil and weather, from accumulated technological knowledge, and from accumulated net investment. Productive intelligence derives from heredity and education.

With respect to the materials, it is clear that the more and better the materials a man has, the more he can produce, assuming that he is capable of using the materials. The greater the quantity of land or the more fertile the individual units, the more products a man can grow on it. The more fertilizer a man has, the more he can grow on the land to which the fertilizer is applied. The richer the ore, the more iron he can produce. The bigger the hammer, the more stakes he can drive in an hour (but there are limits: the hammer can be too heavy, or the fertilizer can be too strong). The bigger and better the lathe, the more metal a man can shape in an hour. This is straightforward.

Americans began with higher productivity than Europeans because of rich natural resources. Over time, improvements in technology and growth of per capita physical capital steadily increased the productivity of Americans. Improvements in technology this year and next year, and net investment this year and next year will continue to increase this productivity.

Productive intelligence has also grown over time as nutrition has improved (for example, fresh fruits and vegetables in winter) and as children have stayed in better and better schools for longer periods—until fully one-fourth of all Americans are at least 21 years old before they leave school. E. F. Denison, America's leading authority on United States economic growth, has attributed 40% of the nation's 1929 to 1957 growth in output per hour to improved productive intelligence.[1]

What is productive intelligence? It is the whole range of human physical and mental abilities valued in the marketplace Most emphatically, it includes ambition. The determinants of individual productive intelligence may be more conveniently studied if the word "intelligence" is (1) restricted to behavior valued in the marketplace, and (2) subdivided to be applied to three different time periods in each person's life. Doing this, we can distinguish between Intelligence A, the individual's marketable potential at the moment of conception, Intelligence B, the individual's marketable potential at the moment of birth, and Intelligence C, the individual's marketable ability at any point in life after birth.

Intelligence A is a limiting concept. The genes that join in the sperm and egg may carry the potential for a mathematical genius or may limit the individual so narrowly that he will be unable to learn to write, count, or even speak. Barring as yet unknown processes in surgery and biology, the person with defective genes cannot be lifted out of idiocy. He is doomed to zero production.

Babies with low Intelligence A cannot rise. Babies with high Intelligence A may not rise. Kept in a room with blank walls and from contact with other people, an individual with an Intelligence A potential for mathematical genius will, nevertheless, be an idiot who is unable to talk or count, much less create new concepts. If he had been given an appropriate education, he would have become a creative master of mathematical concepts; but, uneducated, he has no productive ability.

Intelligence A refers to all kinds of marketable productive potential: ability to count, to persuade, to organize production, to teach, to use a shovel, to write novels, and to assemble transistor radios. The list is very long. We may think of Intelligence A as a single measure comprised of thousands of different kinds of potential ability, or we may conceive of there being many Intelligence A's, one for each kind of ability potential.

---

[1] E. F. Denison, *The Sources of Economic Growth in the United States,* Committee for Economic Development, New York, N.Y., 1962, p. 73.

For each kind of marketable ability, Intelligence A is the genetic potential at the time of conception. This genetic potential may or may not be realized—that will depend upon events affecting the individual after conception. But the genetic potential, given the present state of biological-medical knowledge, can never be surpassed.

Between the time of conception and the time of birth, a great deal can happen that will lower an individual's potential. The devastating effects upon the baby of German measles in the mother during the second month of pregnancy are well known.

Millenia have favored the reproduction of genes of women who bore children over the genes of women who did not. Through the years, modern women have become endowed with a body chemistry that will sacrifice its own welfare to protect and preserve the baby. During the nine months between conception and birth, the mother's body will do all it can but, sometimes, the mother's body cannot do all that is needed. Malnutrition, incompatible Rh factor combination, and physical mistreatment can cripple the ability of the mother's body to serve the needs of the fetus. Then the baby may die or its Intelligence B may suffer. Intelligence B may be cut below the potential granted in Intelligence A at the time of conception.

The child's intellectual potential can be eroded by maternal malfunctioning or by the malfunctioning of those attending the delivery. In extreme cases, infants die; in less severe instances, the babies suffer cerebral palsy, mental retardation, epilepsy, or other neurologic disorders.[2] In these cases, Intelligence B and, later, Intelligence C suffer.

The erosion of infants' Intelligence A, caused by incompetence or by inadequate care during obstetrical period, can be avoided by mothers who have access to proper food, shelter, security, and medical care before and during delivery. This evasion is more difficult for poor women. The lower the socioeconomic group of the mother, the further is the Intelligence B of her baby likely to be cut below the baby's Intelligence A and the

---

[2] Benjamin Pasamanick and Hilda Knobloch, "Some Thoughts on the Inheritance of Intelligence," *The American Journal of Orthopsychiatry*, July 1961, pp. 454–473.

more likely is the poverty of the parents to be passed on to the children.

After birth, environment begins to operate directly, rather than through the mother, on each person. Intelligence C is the summary combination of environment with heredity. Much of Intelligence C derives from formal schooling: grade school, junior high school, high school, college, and university, for example. But much of Intelligence C comes from the home, relatives, and friends in years before school as well as during the school years. These people can teach the child to be polite or impolite, to be ambitious, complacent, or despairing, to want to be a friar or nun sworn to poverty, or a worthy successor to the father as president of the company, a policeman, or a taunter of police, expert with the switchblade.

The importance of the home can be emphasized by imagining the case of two people beginning with equal Intelligence A but attaining unequal Intelligence C because their families are different. Imagine two male babies with high and equal Intelligence A conceived on the same day in 1946, one to a Negro share-cropper in Sunflower County, Mississippi, the other to a white senior partner in a firm of CPA's and living in Oak Park, Illinois, Grosse Point, Michigan, Shaker Heights, Ohio, Darien, Connecticut, or some other equally comfortable suburb. Trapped in a cotton county with barbarously primitive schools, the Negro boy would be educated quite differently from the white surburbanite. We could safely bet 10,000 to 1 that, despite precisely equal Intelligence A, the two boys would have very dissimilar Intelligence C. The white boy would be superior in nearly all the kinds of Intelligence C that are valued highly in the market.

While accumulating Intelligence C, individuals enter the market. There, all things equal, their share of the national product is as large as their contribution to its making.

III. THE PERFECTLY FUNCTIONING MARKET ECONOMY

One man's perfection is another man's failure. As used here, "perfect" means that physical capital is privately owned, that education and physical capital are distributed among men in a way that maximizes their efficiency, that no one has monopoly power, that men go to work in the jobs in which they are most productive, and that the output is divided in unqualified accord with the principle "to each according to his contribution to production." This can be called "the perfectly functioning market economy of competitive private enterprise."

To attain maximum efficiency, how are physical capital and education to be divided? (It is convenient here to think of medical care as one aspect of physical capital and education.) If educational resources and physical capital were unlimited, everyone's potential could be fully developed and utilized. However, educational resources and physical capital are not unlimited; they can be used to permit an individual to approach but not to reach his full potential. The perfect market, from its limited stock, will give to each individual an education (and physical capital to work with) up to that point at which his added productivity from his last unit of training (or of physical capital) is exactly the same as the added productivity from the last unit of education (or of physical capital) given to his neighbor. These extra products are exactly equal to the added production from the last unit of education (or of physical capital) given to every other individual. This distribution of education and physical capital maximizes potential output.

Having thus allocated education and physical capital, the perfect market moves men into the positions—as employees *or* as employers—in which they can be most productive. To achieve this, the market must provide each person with perfect knowledge of the existing alternatives and with perfect mobility to the most attractive positions. The perfect market then pays the men in those positions in proportion to their contributions to production.

The market economy of competitive private enterprise works perfectly when education and training are accessible to those who can use them most productively; when tools, buildings, land, and materials are available to those who can best use them; and when each person knows of all work opportunities and is able to move to the one where he is most productive. These conditions are conceivable; they are not attainable. If they were attained, the competitive private enterprise market economy would function perfectly and each person would be paid in proportion to his contribution to production.[3]

The United States is a market economy, but does not function (by the present definition) "perfectly." Some departures from perfection are technologically forced; for example, it is physically impossible for every person to know of every job. Some departures are voluntary; Americans choose to tax themselves and give the money to the blind and to the physically disabled. Despite the many departures from perfection, an approximation of the American economy can be made based on generalizations drawn from a market that allocates resources to maximize output and distributes income in proportion to productive contribution. The concept of the perfectly functioning market economy of competitive private enterprise is *not* an ideal to be sought; it is a model which, when understood, helps an observer to comprehend the economy of the United States.

IV. THE PERFECT MARKET, HEREDITY AND POVERTY

American economists conclude that the most productive economy and the one providing the maximum of personal freedom to its members is a market economy based upon private ownership and competition—with extra market provision made for those who otherwise would go hungry. In this market, education and physical capital move to their most productive uses; output is divided—almost—in proportion to productive contribution; and some people are left poor. Some are poor because of inferior inheritance; others are poor because of unfortunate events occurring after conception.

The perfect market would split the national product in proportion to ownership of Intelligence C and property: buildings, machinery, materials, land, and intangibles (such as patents and trademarks) used in production. Some persons would begin with more productive property than others because some parents leave larger inheritances than others. To some observers, this inherited-property inequality will appear inequitable. Some

---

[3] For a more complete description of this model, see Robert Haveman and Kenyon Knopf, *The Market System*, in this series.

who call this unjust will have inherited superior Intelligence A but will *not* call unjust the inequality of inherited Intelligence A. The chief difference between inheriting superior Intelligence A and inheriting superior quantities of land and other physical capital is that physical capital can be transferred to someone else; Intelligence A cannot. Both inherited superiorities, left undisturbed, lead to superior incomes.

Perhaps a system would be more equitable if everyone started with the same physical assets and the same Intelligence A. They do not. Without making a value judgment, the perfectly functioning market economy of· competitive private enterprise accepts this inequality, uses each person and his assets in proportion to his ability to produce, and divides the output in proportion to the productive contribution of the intelligence and assets of each.

The primary points are: (1) that the perfectly functioning market economy of competitive private enterprise results in income inequality as wide as the inequalities in Intelligence A and physical assets; and (2) that those persons with the least physical assets and the lowest Intelligence A will be left poor by such a system. Among the poor of the United States, there are many who are poor because of inferior inheritance. They would be poor even if the market were perfect in the sense here used. Many of the poor of the United States are poor for other reasons.

V. THE PERFECT MARKET, MISFORTUNE, AGE, AND POVERTY

Deficient inheritance in physique, mentality, and property leaves many people poor in a perfectly functioning market economy. Such people are poor, as the previous section explained, because deficient inheritance allows them to produce little, and those who produce little in the market receive small shares of the product. There is a second reason for poverty in the perfectly functioning market economy. It is low productivity resulting from age or from the misfortunes of accident, disease, and mental illness. These factors may restrict their victims to producing so little that they receive small pieces of output. In 1960, there were in the United States more than 100 thousand blind persons, 500 thousand permanently and totally disabled, 800 thousand people in mental hospitals (on any one day), and 700 thousand in other hospitals (on any one day), a total of 2.1 million people. Many among these 2.1 million unfortunates were the victims of the hereditary misfortunes mentioned in the preceding section. Most of these were rendered unproductive by at least one of the numerous misfortunes to which man is subject after conception.

With notable exceptions (Homer and James Thurber were both marvelously productive while blind), the 2.1 million people in the four categories had productivity near zero. Millions of other Americans have suffered lesser reductions in personal productivity because of physical illness, psychic disorder, or physical injury, yet many of these have suffered reductions great enough to confine their productivity below the poverty line. The numbers of these people are large but uncounted.

Because of the nature of man, extended periods of low-to-zero productivity are forced upon him as he matures and as he ages. Asked by the Sphinx, "What is that which is four-footed, two-footed, and three-footed?" Oedipus drove the monster to suicide by correctly answering, "Man, for as a child, he crawls on four feet; as an adult, he walks on two; and as an old man, he adds a cane." By his nature, man is unproductive while on four feet and for some years thereafter; and he is unproductive when on three feet, and often, for many years before.

In July of 1963, there were among the 188.5 million resident Americans, 68.7 million persons of age 17 or younger, and 17.5 million persons of age 65 or older. Winston Churchill was 65 when he became prime minister in 1940; Shirley Temple was an American household word when she was 7. But these were exceptions. About 80 to 90% of the youth and elderly people in the United States produce very little, and are poor when not allowed to share in the earned income of other people. This largely explains why there were 4.7 million persons over age 64 and 15 million persons under age 18 among the 34.1 million people counted as poor by the SSA criteria after allowing for the assets of the elderly. Thus, among the total population in 1963, 46% were above 64 or under 18, while among the 34.1 million poor that year, 58% were in either category.

VI. SUMMARY

The amount of poverty in a nation depends upon the size of its GNP and the way in which GNP is distributed. The GNP of the United States has trebled since 1929. Despite great population growth, per capita GNP has nearly doubled.

The larger the portion of GNP taken by the public sector, the less portion there is available to the private sector. The federal share is largest during war; but, since 1952, the federal share has declined just a little less than the state and local share has grown, so that the private share has, since 1956, remained at about 80% of GNP.

The private share is divided between investment and consumption. The greater the consumption share, the lower the incidence of poverty can be in the current year. The greater the investment share, the lower the incidence of poverty can be in future years. Since 1945, about one sixth of America's total product has gone to investment while more than five eighths of it has gone to consumption. Per capita gross investment has fluctuated over time, but has remained high enough to permit the doubling of per capita consumption which, since 1932, has greatly reduced the incidence of poverty in the United States.

As American national product is being divided between public and private sectors, and as the private sector's share is being divided between consumption and investment, consumption and title to the investment portions are being distributed among members of the total population. The present American system of distribution works in the sense that only a few Americans favor fundamental change in the basic system.

Yet the present American system of distribution is not the only one possible. Three other methods have been described briefly: (1) perfect equality, with every person receiving exactly the same amount as every other person; (2) authoritarianism-traditionalism, with those in authority distributing output according to tradition and personal fiat; and (3) distribution according to need so that the last unit of output going to each person satisfies exactly the same intensity of personal need as the last unit going to every other person. If the United States were peacefully converted to either the first or the third alternative, there would be no poverty in the United States—although total output might be down.

America's present system of distribution is generally characterized by the principle, "To each according to his productive contribution." This is the general rule. Market imperfections, charity, and tax-transfer arrangements provide exceptions to the rule by providing many people with more than their productive contribution while leaving others with less.

Given the general rule, productive intelligence is of primary importance in determining the distribution of output. In this chapter the term intelligence has been confined to abilities valued in the marketplace and has been subdivided to be applied at three time periods in each person's life: in this scheme, Intelligence A refers to genetic potential at the time of conception, Intelligence B to a baby's potential when delivered, and Intelligence C to productive ability at any time after birth.

The perfectly functioning market of competitive private enterprise has been defined as one in which medical care, education, and capital are so allocated among members of the labor force that the last unit going to each person brings forth the same addition to output, and output is distributed in proportion to productive contribution. Such a system of production and distribution would leave some people poor: a portion because of heredity; and others because accident, disease, mental breakdown, or age limited or reduced their Intelligence C, the determinant of output distribution in this system.

This chapter has surveyed the division of the national product among government, investment, and consumption uses and the distribution of consumption and title to net investment as among individuals. The American system of distribution has been described as one tending to distribute output in proportion to productive contribution. If the American market were perfect in the sense of distributing all output according to that rule, there would still be poverty in America. This has been the final theme of this chapter. The next two chapters survey the imperfections—the deviations from the perfect market—that, in the United States, lead to poverty—poverty that would not exist if the market were perfect.

7

Market Imperfections and Poverty

The causes of poverty considered in the preceding chapter—
heredity, accidents, age—derive from conditions and events outside of the market. They would bring on poverty even if the
market economy functioned perfectly. In the abstract sense
used here, the American economy is not perfect, and several
of its imperfections beget poverty which might not exist in
a perfect market.

One market imperfection that causes poverty is racial discrimination. Discrimination prevents the development of Intelligence C in the individuals who are its objects. Discrimination also prevents the productive application of any Intelligence
C that might, nevertheless, develop in these individuals. Undeveloped and unused potential results in low productivity and
in income below the poverty line. The effects are quantitatively
so extensive that the entire next chapter is devoted to an analysis
of discrimination as a cause of poverty.

Many market imperfections alleviate or eliminate some of
the poverty that would exist in a perfectly functioning market
economy. These imperfections are considered in later chapters.
This chapter considers market imperfections that cause or
aggravate poverty. These imperfections are grouped under six
headings; the first of these is misallocation of educational resources.

I. MISALLOCATION OF EDUCATIONAL RESOURCES

No matter how great the mechanical, literary, managerial, artistic, or leadership potential of the newly conceived person, denial of education (or obstetrical care) will prevent the potential from being realized and applied in the marketplace. Thus, according to Thomas Gray:

> Full many a flower is born to blush unseen,
> And waste its sweetness on the desert air.
> And in the country churchyard, there is laid
> Some heart once pregnant with celestial fire;
> Hands, that the rod of empire might have sway'd,
> Or wak'd to extasy the living lyre.
> But knowledge to their eyes her ample page
> Rich with the spoils of time did ne'er unroll;
> Chill Penury repress'd their noble rage,
> And froze the genial current of the soul.[1]

In a perfectly functioning market economy, education goes to those who can best put it to prodctive use in manufacturing, mining, construction, finance, agriculture, commerce, the professions, or the arts. Education is misallocated when a relatively great marginal productive potential in one man is left undeveloped while a relatively minor one is developed in another.

In the United States educational misallocation is widespread and takes many forms, but there are no precise quantitative measures. One statistic is partially relevant. In 1965, there were about 7.3 million Americans past the age of 24 (7% of all adults past 24) who were "functional illiterates." They had failed to complete the fifth grade and, in consequence, had little to offer in the marketplace. Some of these did not have the Intelligence B that would have justified keeping them in school beyond the fourth grade. Most of them did have that ability but were victims of educational misallocation.

Misallocation of educational resources also occurs at more advanced levels. Every experienced college professor has known dozens of students with minimal Intelligence B who, never-

---

[1] *Elegy Written in a Country Churchyard*, Heritage Press, New York, 1951, pp. 12–14.

theless, tried to get through college because their financially able parents insisted on their acquiring a bachelor's degree. On the other hand, experienced high school teachers report many cases of students who fail to go to college, or even to complete high school, even though they have high Intelligence B. This information is impressionistic and has not been quantified, but we may assume that most school dropouts represent educational misallocation—often because of a lack of ambition in the young.

Ambition, like literacy, is acquired by learning. In the present context, ambition means motivation for economic achievement. For several decades, American psychologists have been examining the childhood origins of this kind of achievement motivation. They have discovered a great deal about the character of achievers and about the environments in which achievement motivation is learned.[2] Most Americans do learn achievement motivation, and work to develop the Intelligence C's most valued in the market. Many, however, fail to develop useful Intelligence C's because their environments never teach them to work to develop the kinds of Intelligence C that the market values. When an individual fails to learn *this* kind of ambition, he is pointed toward low productivity and poverty. A proper allocation of educational resources would prevent this outcome.

Educational resources are also misallocated when individuals are miseducated, that is to say, when they receive training they will not apply. High school training in agriculture is a case in point. Many official "Future Farmers of America" are not future farmers. In 1950 there were in the United States about 5.4 million farms and almost 765 thousand high school vocational agriculture students; in 1961, there were 3.7 million farms and 805 thousand vocational agricultural students. Many of the 805 thousand students were spending months learning skills they would never use.

Miseducation also results from changes in technology and consumption patterns. On-the-job training plays a major role in the American educational system, and is often narrowly specialized

---

[2] See, for example, David C. McClelland, *The Achieving Society*, Van Nostrand, Princeton, N.J., 1961.

training for a particular job with a particular employer. When technology or consumption patterns change, some men with specialties are left high and dry, educated in an obsolete skill. The carriagemakers and glassblowers are famous examples; the bituminous coal mining force is, in part, a recent example. Agriculture is a current case, and is discussed further a little later on. Once jobs change, the only education that counts is education that is appropriate to the new production techniques. Education involving an obsolete technique is scarcely better than no education at all.

Finally, misallocation of educational resources results when information regarding occupational and job choices does not reach present and prospective workers. The perfectly functioning market economy requires that each individual know of all available jobs—by occupation, industry, and geographic location. If each individual is to move to that one job in which he is most productive, information about opportunities is almost as important as literacy. Most Americans, both before and after they enter the labor force, know little about occupational and job possibilities. Many youths select their occupations under parental pressure, forced to follow a parent's calling. Sometimes this is the best occupational choice for the child (he has, after all, been learning the trade at the dinner table since infancy); sometimes it is not.

Most Americans, knowing little of opportunities, choose jobs through the "buddy system." Newspaper ads and employment service agencies are secondary. The typical American chooses a job because a buddy (friend or relative) tells him of its availability. This means that the typical American's knowledge of job opportunities is limited to what his friends and relatives know. This is far short of the ideal.

Ignorance of choice is more than a matter of not knowing what options exist today. The slogan "You can't get tomorrow's jobs with today's skills" emphasizes the importance of also knowing how the labor market of the future will differ from the labor market of the present. To the extent that a future job requires lengthy training, the prospective jobholder must know what the future market will be like so that he can begin the prerequisite training in time to be qualified when the new job opens. Again the buddy system is, in the 1960's, the chief determinant of most individuals' expectations regarding the future. And, again, knowledge falls short of the ideal.

People ignorant of the choices today work in jobs where their productivity is so restricted as to leave them below the poverty line. If they were aware of other opportunities, many could move to jobs where their productivity and income would rise above the poverty line. People ignorant of impending change in their present jobs are not currently training in the skills that would maximize their productivity in the future. Unprepared for the change, some of these people will drop below the poverty line when change comes. If they knew of prospective changes, they could begin to train now for the future.

How much poverty does misallocation of educational resources cause? There is no precise answer. Some of the statistics in Chapter 2 are partially relevant. Using the $2999 poverty criterion, the Bureau of the Census counted 9.7 million poor families in 1959. Men aged 25 to 64 headed 4.5 million of these families. Among these 4.5 million male family heads, 709 thousand were high school dropouts and about 3 million left school before finishing ninth grade. Some of these men with little schooling had Intelligence B too low to justify further education. Others had Intelligence B so high that the society would have benefitted from a larger share of educational resources going to them. If that had happened, there might have been much less poverty in America in 1963.

Misallocation of educational resources refers to the use of a fixed quantity of physical and human educational resources. Misallocation is corrected, and efficiency is maximized by transferring resources so that some people receive more education while other people receive less education than under conditions of misallocation. Chapters 10 and 11 examine both misallocation and the proper division of the NNP between education and all other uses. Each person must decide for himself what constitutes a proper division. This can be done subjectively by comparing the costs with the gains that would follow if a larger (or smaller) share of NNP were to go to education.

The previous chapter cited the case of a Negro sharecropper's son and a northern white CPA's son conceived on the same day with identical Intelligence A. By reallocating educational resources from their customary channels to provide more to the sharecropper's son and less to the CPA's son, both boys could become nonpoor. Or the Negro could avoid poverty if more of the NNP were devoted to his education while less went into the production of beer, milk, or penicillin. By reallocating fixed educational resources *or* by devoting more of NNP to education, much of today's poverty could be erased. Chapters 10 and 11 consider pertinent issues in deciding whether changes should be made.

II. UNWILLINGNESS TO CHANGE

Another market imperfection causing poverty is a man's unwillingness to change from a position of low productivity (on a small farm) or chronic unemployment (in Appalachian coal mining) to an area and position of maximized productivity. Contemplating occupational change, some men are eager to move to more productive positions, but others refuse to change, saying, "I can't change; this work is in my blood" or "I'm too old to change." Contemplating geographic change, some men are eager to move, for some express the classic wish, "I sure would like to move anywhere far away from my mother-in-law." Others say, "I'm too old to move" or "All my friends and relatives are here; I can't leave them" or "I just can't see taking my kids away from the country and making them live in the city." [3]

These immobile people refuse to change, although they know of alternatives. Other people do not change because they do not know of alternatives; this latter group was considered in the preceding section. The people who refuse to move are very much like people without ambition. Both groups refuse to respond to market opportunities that would maximize their productivity and income. Thus, they refuse to behave as "good citizens" of a market economy. Presumably, they were not born market misfits. They must have failed to learn to respond to

---

[3] Alan B. Batchelder, "Occupational and Geographic Mobility: Two Ohio Area Case Studies," *Industrial and Labor Relations Review*, July 1965, pp. 581–582.

the inducements of the market, or perhaps they were taught to disdain market forces. Viewed in these terms, refusal to move to more productive locations or occupations is, like failure of ambition, another instance of misallocation of educational resources. Nevertheless, people in these categories are generally thought of as being "the undeserving poor."

III. FAMILY OBLIGATIONS

A third market imperfection that causes poverty results from the pressure of family obligations. These obligations keep individuals from attaining above-poverty productivity even though the individuals have an above-poverty productive potential and have access to jobs befitting their potential. Sometimes the individual is a man who must stay home to care for his wife. More often it is a woman with children but with no man in the house; she is unable to leave the children in order to work.

In a variation of this situation, the husband or wife hires someone to care for the dependents but, after paying for the care, there is so little income left that the family falls below the poverty line. If the income of this family were above the poverty line before paying for this care, the family would be counted by the SSA as nonpoor. Families of this kind would be omitted from the poverty count of Chapter 3.

In 1963, 2.8 million United States families with children (10% of all of such families) were headed by a woman. These women, kept from work because of the children, tend largely toward a poverty income, and about 1.6 million of these families were poor in 1963.

IV. THE SOCIAL MINIMUM WAGE

Governments, unions, and businessmen's pride combine to introduce a fourth market imperfection that sometimes aggravates but rarely causes poverty. Governments set minimum wages by establishing laws that forbid employers to pay employees less than a minimum hourly amount. Unions obtain contracts specifying minimum wage levels for each occupation in a plant.

Businessmen set minimum rates that they feel they can, in self-respect, pay employees.

Together, these considerations determine what economist Clarence D. Long (who, since 1962, has been a Maryland Congressman) calls the "social minimum wage," which is a minimum wage that a businessman feels that law, contracts, and self-respect permit him to pay.[4] If this wage is $1.25 per hour, individuals whose productivity is less than $1.25 per hour do not get hired. Instead of a low-earned income in the absence of the social minimum, these least-able people then have a zero earned income—or find work with employers who ignore the social minimum.

If the social minimum wage is $1.25 per hour, which is $2600 for 52 weeks of 40-hours each, people employed at the minimum will, in most cases, have incomes below the poverty line for their household type. Consequently, when a social minimum wage causes unemployment, it does not ordinarily cause poverty. The social minimum wage aggravates poverty by moving some families from a high-poverty earned income to the deeper-poverty income of unemployment.

V. RISING PRODUCTIVITY

Rising productivity is the chief instrument by which poverty previously has been reduced in the United States, and is the chief instrument by which poverty will be reduced in the future. Yet, rising productivity, in combination with market imperfections of ignorance, geographic-occupational immobilities, or deficient demand, can cause poverty. Is this a paradox? Indeed, it is!

Rising productivity derives, first, from an increase in the per capita quantity of physical or human capital and, second, from improvement in the quality of capital. Quality improvements are called technological change. Automation involves some special cases of technological change where machines are tied together in sequence or arranged to check and correct one another for purposes of quality control.

---

[4] C. D. Long, "An Overview of Postwar Labor Market Developments," in *Proceedings of the 4th Annual Social Security Conference*, W. E. Upjohn Institute, Kalamazoo, 1962.

All automation is technological change, but not all technological change is automation. All technological change raises productivity, but not all rising productivity derives from technological change. As far as poverty is concerned, all cases of automation, all cases of technological change, and all cases of rising productivity open the *same* opportunities.

The following example of early technological change and capital accumulation illustrates the options opened up by every case of increased productivity.

Once there were two men, Abel and Seth.[5] They were helping to build a temple to their God and were piling up a great mound of earth on which priests would arrange the stones for the temple. To carry the dirt, they assembled a platform by fastening 30-inch poles crosswise between the middle 36 inches of two 7-foot poles. Abel stood between the two long poles at one end, and Seth at the other, the platform of cross-poles being in the middle. Using this tool, Abel and Seth could carry their combined weight in earth on the platform.

Plodding back and forth for a few days, the two men saw the pile of dirt gradually get higher. Estimating, carefully, they predicted that the pile could be completed in 1 year (24 man-months of work) if both men worked 8 hours a day for 7 days a week.

That same day, Abel invented the wheel and axle, and Seth invented the wheelbarrow. Temporarily, both men gave up earth-moving and worked on the wheel and axle. They fastened the wheel and axle to one end of their platform, added sides, and had a wheelbarrow.

The construction of the wheel, axle, and wheelbarrow took 1 month of each man's time, but the time seemed to have been well spent, since it permitted 1 man to carry heavier loads than 2 men could carry before. Reestimating, Abel and Seth concluded that the pile of dirt could now be finished in 10 months by only 1 man working 8-hour days for 7 days a week.

Arithmetic can now be used to survey the possibilities opened up by the introduction of the wheelbarrow. Before the wheelbarrow, the completion of the dirt pile required that 2 men

---

[5] My thanks go to Charles W. Mann who originated this illustration.

work 12 months—a total of 24 months of labor. After the technological change, the completion of the dirt pile required 2 months of labor (to produce the wheelbarrow) plus 10 months of labor with the wheelbarrow in use—a total of 12 months of labor. Technological change had increased productivity by 100%.

Given the 100% increase in productivity, Seth and Abel could choose from four distinct ways of reaping the fruits of higher productivity.

First, they could both continue to haul dirt for 8 hours a day; they would have to work in shifts so that each could enjoy unrestricted access to the wheelbarrow during his 8 hours. In 5 months beyond the 1 month used to make the wheelbarrow, they would complete the dirt pile; in another 6 months (they would have to make a second wheelbarrow) they could complete a second dirt pile. Their first choice was to continue the same amount of work and to double the dirt piles in 24 man-months of labor.

Second, they could continue working 8 hours a day for 7 days a week and finish the dirt pile in 12 man-months of labor; then, they could use 12 months of labor to cut stones for the temple, carry messages, or do other things. Their second choice was the same amount of dirt in half the work time with the other half devoted to producing other goods or services.

Third, they could each work 4 hours a day—again, in alternate shifts. With half the number of works hours required before the wheelbarrow, they could complete the dirt pile in 10 more months. The third choice was the same amount of dirt with half as much work and more leisure.

Fourth, Seth could be laid off. In 10 more 8-hour-a-day, 7-day-a-week months, Abel could complete the dirt pile; during the 12th month, he would be laid off. The 4th choice was the same amount of dirt with half the labor force, the rest of the labor force being unemployed.

Whenever productivity doubles, an economy must choose among the following four things.

Option 1. Double the product.
Option 2. The same product plus other goods and services.
Option 3. The same product with one half of the work per man.
Option 4. The same product with one half of the employed.

Of course, productivity never rises 100% so quickly as in our example. Thirty three years must elapse before it doubles in the United States, but a productivity increase of 20%, 2%, or ·0.2% opens up these same four kinds of possibilities. The people working or buying in a market economy decide which course shall be taken; more precisely, they decide which combination of the four courses will be activated.

If working hours are halved for each person (Option 3), the output remains the same. Individual shares and poverty are unchanged. Each person has increased leisure to add to his unchanged share of product. If everyone continues to work the same hours (Options 1 and 2), output can double, and there will be twice as much for everyone. This had been the historical route to reducing the amount of poverty. People with relatively small shares before the change may have relatively small shares after it, but in absolute size, their shares may be twice as big afterward. Thus, the poor cease to be poor. However, the course of laying off half the workers (Option 4) may be chosen. This leaves the working half with the same total output but twice the share per person. This option, although lifting some who had low income to above poverty levels, plunges the unemployed half into deepest poverty.

Over the long run, the American economy has chosen a bit more leisure each decade and a larger quantity of output per person. There has been *no* increase in unemployment since 1925, or since 1900, or 1850, or 1800. Output per man hour has gone up at least tenfold since 1800; yet the unemployment rate has not gone up at all.

In the short run, rising productivity does make some Americans poor. This happens whenever ignorance of choices, lack of access to education, unwillingness to change, or deficient demand leads to the option of unemployment (or underemployment) for some people. Agriculture is a striking example of the way in which rising productivity can reduce national poverty while causing short-run, localized poverty.

Between 1929 and 1965 real product per man hour rose more than 100% in American agriculture (for more detail, see Table 10-3). If the Seth-and-Abel example were shifted from temple building to agriculture, their productivity increase would mean that Seth could produce more food and fiber in a 1965 hour than he and Abel together could have produced in a 1929 hour. This kind of productivity increase (as Chapter 4 observed) has reduced the incidence of poverty in America by raising the output per hour of the average worker.

Responding to greater agricultural productivity, Americans took a bit more food per person and a lot more of many other things (Option 2), but they did not choose 100% more food per person or any amount near a 100% increase. To adjust to rising productivity by switching to the production of other products, many "Seths" had to leave farming for nonagricultural work. Many of them went to the cities to manufacture the agricultural equipment that has increased agricultural productivity. Most of them took other city jobs.

When the first American census was taken in 1790, 5% of all Americans lived in urban areas (towns of 2500 or more people). The other 95% lived on farms. Over every decade since 1790, the *percentage* engaged in farming has decreased. Since World War I, the *number* of people on American farms has decreased persistently. In 1920, the United States farm population was about 32 million; by 1960, it had dropped to 16 million, and by 1964 it was down to almost 13 million.

This decline has been rapid, but not rapid enough. Ignorance of choices, lack of access to education, unwillingness to change —especially among older farmers—and years of deficient demand have kept many Seths from leaving farming. These Seths experience unemployment or, more often, "underemployment" by working "poverty farms." What is "underemployment" on "poverty farms?"

The farms run by the "Abels" are big and well suited to the new equipment and the new techniques. Around these big farms there remains other farm land. But when this leftover land is divided among the numerous Seths, the resulting farms are often too small (and, sometimes, too hilly) to permit use of the new farming equipment and techniques. Whether or not the Seths use modern farming methods, their superfluous numbers confine them to "poverty farms"—farms too small to yield outputs that would achieve the net incomes of the Abels who use the new equipment and the new techniques on large farms. It is as though Abel worked with the new wheelbarrow while

Seth, after being laid off the wheelbarrow job, insisted on en-
listing another man to help him carry dirt on the old two-man
hand-carried platform. Alternatively, it is as though Abel used
the wheelbarrow for full loads while Seth insisted on using it
for half loads. In either case Seth's income is only one half of
Abel's.

Some Seths are so limited by heredity or irreversible mis-
fortune that their Intelligence C could never lift them above
poverty incomes. But many Seths could earn their way out of
poverty if they would leave their poverty farms for other work.
Such men are underemployed when on poverty farms. If most
of them would give up farming, the high Intelligence C Seths
remaining could obtain enough land to become Abels.

In the meantime (as Table 3-1 showed), 25% of all farm
families lived in poverty in 1963. However, because relatively
few Americans lived on farms in 1963, less than 10% of all poor
persons lived on farms.

Rural poverty can be reduced by decreasing the number of
Seths on poverty-size farms. But the superfluous Seths can get
out of farming only if aggregate demand provides a market
large enough to absorb the increased quantity of goods and
services they can produce if freed by rising productivity. This
is true of agriculture and of all the other industries in which
rising physical output per man hour enables toilers to produce
additional goods and services.

VI. DEFICIENT DEMAND: OVERALL
MARKET IMPERFECTION

Thus far, the discussion has dealt with market imperfections
caused by educational deficiencies, unwillingness to change
location or jobs, family obligations, and the social minimum
wage. These imperfections keep people unemployed or in
inferior jobs while jobs exist in which they could be more productive. Also these imperfections cause structural unemployment or underemployment among particular portions of the
population or in particular areas of the country. On the other
hand, deficient demand is a market imperfection that involves
the entire economy.

When demand is deficient, three of its consequences cause

poverty. First, people unemployed for long periods drop into poverty (those who are unemployed for as much as two or three months between jobs can still earn above poverty incomes for the year). Second, people who can obtain only part-time work drop into poverty. Third, people who in a full-employment economy would have high-productivity jobs but who can obtain only low-productivity jobs because of deficient demand may also drop into poverty.

A growing labor force adds to a nation's potential NNP, as does rising productivity. If aggregate demand increases more rapidly than productivity and the labor force, the incidence of poverty will decrease. Conversely, if aggregate demand rises less rapidly than the labor force and productivity (or if aggregate demand decreases), the incidence of poverty will rise.

Aggregate demand varies in response to many variables. Several statistics can provide examples of changes in variables that are immediately associated with variation in aggregate demand. Between 1929 and 1932 gross private investment decreased from $17 to $1.1 billion a year and the incidence of poverty soared. Between 1939 and 1944, federal spending rose $86.6 billion while federal tax collections rose only $34.3 billion in the national product accounts. The incidence of poverty was cut sharply as expansive fiscal policy and permissive monetary policy shaved unemployment to 1.2% of the civilian labor force. Between 1946 and 1948, fiscal policy was restrictive, monetary policy was permissive, and unleashed pent-up demand for marriages, babies, and consumer durables held aggregate demand up.

In every year federal monetary and fiscal policies push up or down on aggregate demand. Together these policies contributed to the great contraction of 1929 to 1933, to the wavering 1930's, to the soaring wartime recovery, and so on into the limping 1950's and early 1960's when balance-of-payments considerations inhibited use of expansive monetary and fiscal policy. Applied aggressively beginning with the 1964 tax cut, expansive monetary and fiscal policy had cut unemployment from 6.8% of the civilian labor force in February 1961 to 3.7% in February 1966.

Always, federal monetary and fiscal policies confront a dilemma. The less expansive these policies are, the higher the unemployment and poverty rates will be. The more expansive these policies are, the more rapidly will prices rise. This dilemma is examined in more detail in the final two chapters of this book.

VII. SUMMARY

In Chapter 6 we examined poverty resulting from low productivity in a perfectly functioning market economy. The present chapter has described market imperfections causing poverty that would not exist in a perfectly functioning market economy (imperfections preventing some of the poverty of the perfect market have not yet been considered; they are discussed in Chapter 9).

In summary, the market imperfection called misallocation of educational resources takes many forms as a cause of poverty. As manifested in affected individuals, these forms appear as: failure to learn ambition; failure to continue in school; inappropriate education; education for jobs that have disappeared; or minimal education regarding present and future job possibilities. If educational resources were properly allocated, other things being equal, the people affected by misallocation could move into jobs that maximized their productivity. By doing so, many of these people would move from below to above the poverty line.

Since the children of the poor are least likely to have access to the better schools, or to an environment teaching achievement motivation, or to information regarding job opportunities, misallocation of educational resources tends to perpetuate the poverty of parents in their children. When medical care and medical information skimp the poor, babies with equal Intelligence A are born with unequal Intelligence B and, once more, poverty is perpetuated in the children of poor parents.

The "undeserving poor" are a second cause of poverty. They refuse to take the training, jobs, or both that would lift them out of poverty.

A third market imperfection causing poverty is the pressure of family obligations. Most often, this occurs when women head families and cannot work because they cannot leave their small children.

The social minimum wage does not often cause poverty. It can cause unemployment for people who otherwise could be earning below-poverty-line incomes.

Rising productivity, although not itself a deviation from the perfect market, shortens work weeks or frees people from old jobs. People will become unemployed or underemployed and poor (1) if they are ignorant of job opportunities, (2) if they lack access to training needed for other work, (3) if they are unwilling to move or change to other work, or (4) if they face a market characterized by deficient aggregate demand.

Demand is deficient when $C + I + G$ fails to call forth full employment. Federal monetary and fiscal policy can, at the risk of raising prices, provide sufficient demand.

Several market imperfections have now been identified as causes of poverty. Only one of these imperfections remains to be considered; it is discrimination, the subject of the next chapter.

8

The Special Case of Minority Groups

When the first census of the United States was taken in 1790, 19.3% of all Americans were Negroes. By 1963, that percentage was down to 10.9%. Although the portion of the American population composed of Negroes has declined precipitously since 1790, Negro Americans remain the nation's largest minority. Nevertheless, there are other minority groups. Within the comprehensive 1960 census income data for 1959, it is possible to distinguish among Negroes, Indians, Chinese, Japanese, Filipinos, and "other nonwhites." It is also possible to separate statistics for persons of Puerto Rican origin and, in the five southwesternmost states, for persons of Spanish surname.

The superior poverty-counting criteria of the SSA cannot be used for these minorities. The Current Population Survey data, the only statistics to which the SSA criteria have been applied, are based on too small a sample to permit separate poverty counts for any minority. Use of the simple $2999 poverty-income criterion shows a relatively high incidence of poverty among families in four minority groups. Table 8-1 contrasts the low incidence of poverty among families of the white majority with the high incidence of poverty among families of each of these four minority groups and indicates that 23.9% of America's poor families were either Negro, Indian, Puerto Rican, or Mexican-American in 1959.

The SSA poverty criteria would provide a better count but, unfortunately, the Current Population Survey singles out only

Table 8-1 Four Minorities and the White Majority: Number and Percent
of Families with 1959 Income below $3000

Group by Character of Family Head	Number of Families with Incomes in 1959	Within Each Group, Families with 1959 Incomes below $3000	
		Number	Percent
White majority	39,987,000	7,309,000	18.2
Indian	90,560	49,204	54.3
Negro	3,950,316	1,951,765	49.4
Puerto Rican origin	196,607	62,850	32.0
White persons of Spanish surname[a]	698,027	242,903	34.8

[a] In Texas, Arizona, New Mexico, California, and Colorado only.

Source. U. S. Bureau of the Census, *U. S. Census of Population: 1960*,
Government Printing Office, Washington, D.C., 1963, *U. S. Summary*, p. 594;
Nonwhite Population by Race, pp. 25–29; *Puerto Ricans in the United
States*, p. 36; *Persons of Spanish Surname*, p. 36.

one color, racial, or ethnic minority for statistical identification.
This one minority is the color group "nonwhites." In the 1964
Current Population Survey data, the SSA poverty criteria have
been applied to nonwhites. Although there was no poverty count
of Negroes or Indians, comparisons can be made between whites
and nonwhites (all racial terms *are* capitalized; color groups *are
not* capitalized).

For 1959, the simple method counted as poor 18.2% of majority-group white families. In 1963, the SSA criteria counted
as poor only 14.4% of white Americans. Allowances for age,
family size, and farm residence along with the passage of time
and a switch from counting poor white majority-group families
to counting poor white individuals made a big difference
in the estimate of the incidence of poverty among whites.

The simple method counted 49.4% of Negro families and 54.3%
of Indian families as poor in 1965, whereas the SSA criteria
counted 49.3% of nonwhites as poor in 1963. Although the years
and methods differ, the incidence of minority poor by both
counts remains about one half.

The $2999 criterion found that among poor families in 1959,

23.9% belonged to one of four minority groups. Applied to 1963 incomes, the SSA criteria found 1.6 million fewer poor white families but just as many poor nonwhite families as the simple method identified in 1959. Thus, the SSA count found that among the 39.6 million individuals living in poverty in 1963, 30.9% were nonwhites. An educated guess suggests that if the number of poor Puerto Ricans (95% white) and poor white persons of Spanish surname were known, the SSA count would show that among the 1963 poor, 35 to 36% belonged to one of the four minority groups. Because the minority poor constitute so large a portion of the total poor, this entire chapter is devoted to an analysis of the biological, social, and economic relationships that cause this condition.

I. INTELLIGENCE A

To recap briefly: Chapter 7 considered the market imperfections that leave able people poor, and Chapter 6 underscored the point that some people would be left poor by a perfectly functioning market. The perfect market would distribute education and training among individuals in proportion to their Intelligence B; it would distribute physical capital among individuals on the basis of their Intelligence C's capacity to use it, and national output among individuals in proportion to their productive contribution. Moreover, the perfect market would leave poor the people whose productive contribution would be too small to yield a product (and income) above the poverty line and whose product would be low because they would have been conceived with low Intelligence A.

The percentage of poor among Negroes and other minorities is far above the percentage of poor among majority whites. Why the difference? Is it because of racial differences in Intelligence A?

On the average, Negroes are known to be inferior to whites when tested for various Intelligence C's used in the United States market. Do these deficits result because the Intelligence A of minority groups is inferior to that of majority group whites? If the answer to this question is that, on the average, Negroes, Puerto Ricans, Indians, and Mexican-Americans are, at the moment of conception, inferior to the white majority, it follows that the minority groups' greater poverty results from their inherent productive inferiority. Most available evidence compares only Negroes and whites. Although we use Negro-white statistical differences in this chapter, we assume that most of the generalizations also apply to each of the other three minorities.

No one has yet devised a means to measure Intelligence A. Perhaps someday men will be able to measure the genetic intellectual potential of a newly joined sperm and egg. For the present, this remains almost unimaginable.

It is known that some newly conceived whites have the potential to become physicists, theoretical mathematicians, novelists—and even economists—capable of superior achievements. It is also known that some newly conceived Negroes have equally superior potential. This is known because some Negroes and some whites have, in fact, become great physicists, theoretical mathematicians, novelists, and economists. It is known too, that defective genes limit some whites at the moment of conception to a life—usually mercifully short—of idiocy. Some Negroes are similarly doomed from conception.

The market can richly reward members of the former groups if they realize much of their potential, but the market can offer nothing to the members of the latter group who must depend upon relatives, charity, or government aid. However, these are extremes; most persons enter the market near the center. Presumably, the distribution of Intelligence A among whites ranges from retardate to genius following the shape of a nearly normal curve containing most persons near its center. The distribution of Intelligence A among Negroes also ranges from retardate to genius—again, it is assumed, in a nearly normal curve.

How do these two curves compare? There are three possibilities, as Figure 8-1 shows. The means of the curves may be equal; the Negro mean may be inferior to the white mean; or the Negro mean may be superior to the white mean. No one, as yet, knows which of the three sketches is "right." Much is known, however, about factors affecting Intelligence B and Intelligence C.

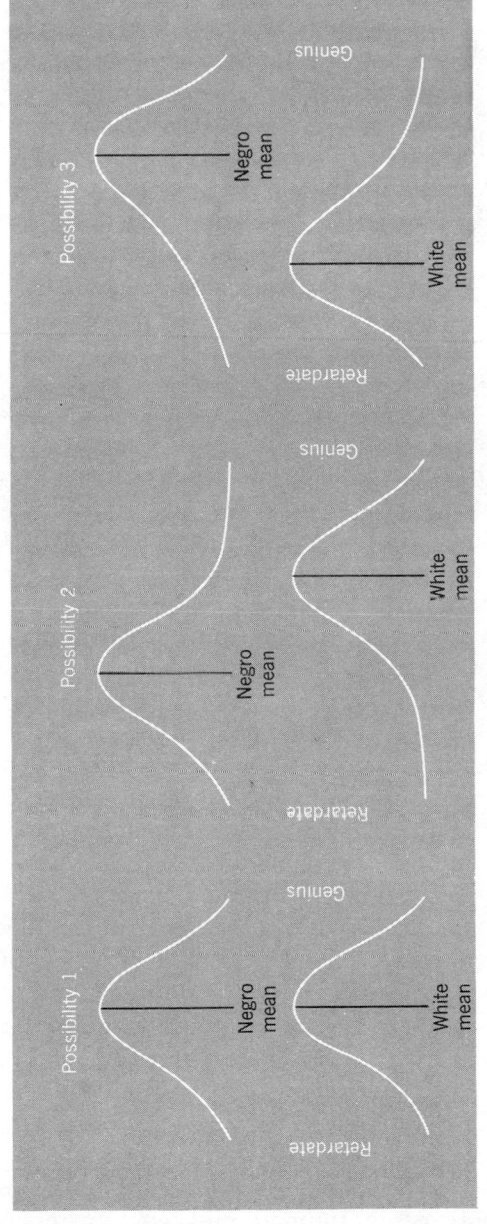

Figure 8-1. Distribution of Intelligence A among Negroes and among whites.

II. INTELLIGENCE B

Chapter 6 included a section describing the manner in which malnutrition, severe emotional stress, and absence of medical attention for expectant mothers could erode the Intelligence A with which their babies were endowed at conception. As a result of such erosion, Intelligence B (an infant's maximum productive potential at birth) would be cut below the fertilized egg's potential at the moment of conception.

Such erosion will not be uniform among infants. Its dangers can be minimized by prospective mothers who have access to proper food, shelter, security, and medical care before and during delivery. We can imagine the manner in which differences in care lead to differences in productive ability.

Suppose it were possible to identify a large number of women who had just conceived. These women could be divided by random selection into two groups called Z and W. During their months of pregnancy, the women in the Group Z could be provided with living conditions that would leave them malnourished, in emotional turmoil, and medically unattended, even during delivery. In contrast, the women in Group W, during pregnancy and delivery, could be provided with living conditions that yielded proper nourishment, emotional security, and good medical attention.

Brain damage and neuropsychiatric disorders would appear in some children of each group, but these misfortunes would be more frequent and more severe among children of the Group-Z mothers than among children of the Group-W mothers. These misfortunes would push Intelligence B further below Intelligence A for the Group-Z children than for the Group-W children. Given equal educational opportunities after birth, the Intelligence C, productive contribution, and income of the Group-Z children would fall further below Intelligence A's promise than would those of the Group-W children.

The hypothetical differences in living conditions between the Group-Z and Group-W mothers strongly suggest actual differences in living conditions between Negro mothers and white mothers in the United States. A larger proportion of prospective Negro mothers go through pregnancy without seeing a doctor. As late as 1963, 10% of nonwhite (0.4% of white) babies were delivered without an attending physician. The absence of an American midwife tradition makes this difference more significant than it would be in Europe.

The results are partly documented. Psychiatrists find that mental deficiency and neuropsychiatric disorders associated with prematurity and complications of pregnancy appear with inordinately high rates among Negroes.[1] These high rates result from the inferior care received by expectant Negro mothers compared with that received by expectant white mothers. Consequently, white mothers, on the average, conserve more of their babies' Intelligence A potential for Intelligence B than do Negro mothers.

III. INTELLIGENCE C

Intelligence A and Intelligence B are concepts relating to particular points in a person's life. Intelligence C can be measured at any point after birth. Whether administered at age 5, 10, 25, or 50, dozens of tests have shown that the Negro average is below the white average in the kinds of Intelligence C highly prized by the American market. On the average, Negroes are inferior to whites but, as Figure 8-2 indicates, the extremes are reached by both whites and Negroes.

The difference in averages could reflect the lower average of Intelligence A among Negroes than among whites. No one knows about this. It is known, however, that the difference in C distributions results, in part, from the difference between whites and Negroes in the availability of proper care during pregnancy and delivery. But this is of relatively minor importance. More important are the differences between Negroes and whites in education and training. Most Americans are aware of the squalid buildings that Mississippi whites (and rural, Southern white school boards, generally) have forced Negroes to use as schools—crowded shacks with cracked wooden black-

---

[1] Benjamin Pasamanick and Hilda Knobloch, "Epidemiologic Studies on the Complications of Pregnancy and the Birth Process," in *Prevention of Mental Disorders in Children*, G. Caplan, ed., Basic Books, New York, 1961, pp. 74–94.

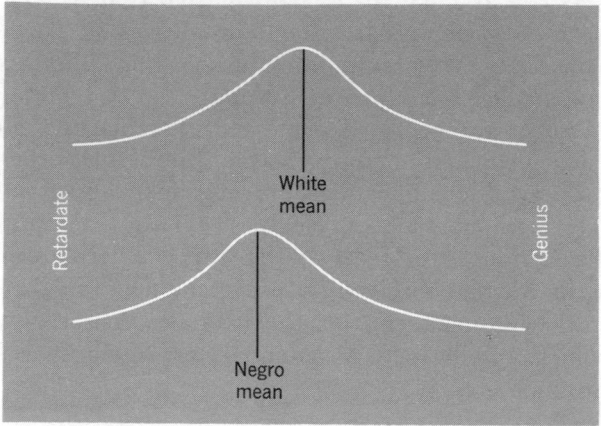

Figure 8-2. Distribution of Intelligence C among whites and among Negroes.

boards, with fewer seats, desks, and books than children, and with poorly educated teachers. Most people also know that city school boards—North, South, East, and West—provide Negro children with buildings, equipment, and teachers inferior to the buildings, equipment, and teachers assigned to white children.[2]

These generalizations are commonplace; their effects are straightforward. Inferior education results in inferior preparation to produce; inferior preparation to produce results in inferior production; and inferior production results in inferior income and a higher incidence of poverty for the group.

The incidence of poverty among Negroes is high at present and is certain to remain high in the future, given the improbability of radical changes in white attitudes and public policy. The certainty of continued high poverty rates among Negroes requires further elaboration here regarding Negro-white differences in Intelligence C in an economy enjoying rapid development.

Economic development takes place when there is an increase

---

[2] Patricia C. Sexton, *Education and Income*, Viking Press, New York, 1961, Chapters 2 and 4 in particular.

in the volume of physical and human capital per member of the labor force. For 150 years, economic development has forged ahead in the United States. If an individual is to benefit from this development, he must have access to the growing stock of physical capital and must be able to use it in his work. He must have access to the training arrangements—at home, in schools, or on the job—by which people acquire human capital (the Intelligence C) required to work with the new physical capital. Having acquired the appropriate Intelligence C, the individual must have the opportunity to apply it in his work. If these conditions are met, an individual will produce more and earn more as economic development progresses in his country.

IV. THE THREE PERIODS

In the United States, whites have had more opportunties than Negroes to participate in economic development. These differences in participation stand out clearly when the American experience is divided into the following three time-space units.

(1) Period One. The South (1793 to 1940), accumulating physical and human capital slowly, kept most American negroes in rural areas cut off from access to the rapidly growing physical and human capital of Northern and Western farms and cities.

(2) Period Two. The South (1940 to date), now rapidly developing, retained most of the American Negro population, but denied it access to the growing physical and human capital of Southern agriculture and manufacturing.

(3) Period Three. The North and West (1917 to date), experiencing persistent economic development, received a steadily growing portion of the Negro population of the United States.

Each period deserves detailed consideration.

A. *The South, 1793 to 1940*

This was the period between the invention of the cotton gin and the large-scale introduction of tractors, cotton cultivators, and cotton pickers into Southern agriculture. During these years, rapid economic development persisted in agriculture and industry outside the South while change was minimal in Southern agriculture.

The need for skilled labor and the availability of Negro talent provided enough economic incentive to induce antebellum planters to train slaves in the Intelligence C's valued in the Southern market. In consequence, slaves did much of the mechanical, engineering, and bookkeeping work of the old South.

One observer reported that in 1865 more than one third of North Carolina's Negroes were engaged in mechanical occupations as blacksmiths, gunsmiths, cabinetmakers, shipbuilders, pilots, and things of this kind. This claim may be exaggerated, but Negro craftsmen were so numerous that the plantation owners' practice of supplying slave mechanics to do urban work provoked numerous petitions from white mechanics to the various Southern state legislatures in protest against the Negro competition. These petitions were generally ignored because the legislation requested would have worked to the disadvantage of the planters who controlled the legislatures.

After the Civil War, the planters had to hire their mechanics and thus lost their economic incentive to favor Negroes over whites. Under the banner of white supremacy, white mechanics were at last able to displace Negroes from skilled work and to keep Negroes from the training required by the crafts. Both before and after the war, most Southern Negroes worked in field agriculture. After the war, the crop lien kept Negro farmers perpetually in debt. White sheriffs kept them from leaving the land while in debt. Together, these institutions bound Negroes to the land almost as effectively as slavery had done before the war.

During Reconstruction, public school systems were introduced into most Southern states. The Redemptionists viewed the Yankee schoolmarms as subversives (to be expelled), and public education (especially in the rural areas) stagnated until the turn of the century. During the twentieth century, public school systems have expanded, but Negroes have been segregated in facilities that have barely qualified for the title, "schools."

The story is told in the official reports of the Mississippi State Department of Education. In 1900, Mississippi school districts spent $8.20 per white child and $2.67 per Negro child for educational costs other than for buildings. For these same purposes, Mississippi in 1940 spent $31.23 per white pupil and $6.69 per Negro pupil. In 1931, Mississippi schools operated 165 days for white children but only 119 days for Negro children. In 1931, there were 706 white high schools and 64 Negro high schools, although there were 30% more Negro children than white children of high school age.

The 1933 to 1935 *Biennial Report* of Mississippi's State Superintendent of Education noted as follows:

Negro teachers in the lower grades frequently have in their charge from seventy-five to one hundred and fifty pupils. . . . Of the 3735 Negro schoolhouses in Mississippi . . . 1440 schools are conducted in churches, lodges, old stores, tenant houses, or whatever building is available. . . . In hundreds of rural Negro schools there are just four blank, unpainted walls, a few old rickety benches, an old stove propped up on brickbats, and two or three boards nailed together and painted black for a blackboard. In many cases, this constitutes the sum total of the furniture and teaching equipment.[3]

The pupils shared discarded textbooks but had no erasers, crayons, extra books, maps, or charts. The Negro children (taught by teachers who were themselves miseducated in segregated schools) confined within this system did not acquire the Intelligence C that white children acquired in public schools. Yet these children grew up and, with their Mississippi "schooling," moved to Northern and Western cities to seek work in the 1960's.

B. *The South, 1940 to Date*

During this second time-space unit, the keynote has been economic development. As long as hand labor was required to weed and thin cotton, there was no incentive to replace it in cotton picking or in planting. Beginning in the early 1940's, all stages of cotton culture were mechanized, and livestock and poultry raising supplemented and partly supplanted cotton farming. The new Southern agriculture demanded additional human capital and larger amounts of physical capital per farm.

To obtain the extra land and new equipment to make a go of

---

[3] Quoted in Senate Committee on the Judiciary, Voting Rights Hearings, 23 March-5 April 1965, 89th, 1st, U.S. Government Printing Office, Washington, D.C., p. 1044.

the new agriculture, farmers needed access to credit. To make effective use of the new equipment, they needed training. Through the Federal Home Board and the system of county agricultural agents, the Federal Government played a primary role in providing credit and instruction to farmers. But the United States Civil Rights Commission found that the Board made loans to whites to buy land and equipment, while making loans to Negroes for food and seed.[4] Loans to whites have permitted increases in the quantity of physical capital per farm. Loans to Negroes have left their capital position unchanged.

There are no statistics showing how willing white Southern bankers have been to lend to Negro farmers for expansion, but the evidence suggests a marked lack of willingness. Between 1930 and 1959, the average size of white Southern farms grew 91% from 130 to 249 acres, while the average Negro farm grew only 21% from 43 to 52 acres.[5] The Civil Rights Commission further found that white agricultural extension agents learned the new techniques as they evolved and taught them to white farmers, while Negro agents continued to teach the same old techniques of cotton culture and home canning (most Negro extension agents also serve as home demonstration agents to housewives).

Without access to the growing stock of physical and human capital needed in the new agriculture, Negroes found that the larger, efficient white farms were pressing prices down and driving them to the margin on their small, ill-equipped farms. With access to training and credit, whites were in a position to buy the distressed Negro farms and the Negroes moved. In 1930, there were 882 thousand Negro farms with about 4.7 million residents. By 1950, there were 559 thousand such farms with 3.2 million residents and, by 1959, there were only 265 thousand of them with almost 1.5 million residents.

Negroes (and whites) left the farms for Southern cities where the number of manufacturing jobs expanded rapidly.

---

[4] U.S. Commission on Civil Rights, *Equal Opportunity in Farm Programs,* U.S. Government Printing Office, Washington, D.C., 1965, pp. 105–107.
[5] U.S. Department of Agriculture, *U.S. Census of Agriculture: 1959,* Vol. II, *General Report,* U.S. Government Printing Office, Washington, D.C., 1962, p. 1035.

Physical capital piled up in urban areas as factories were built to serve the new Southern markets and to be near newly developed raw-material sources and cheap but unskilled labor. Between 1950 and 1960, there was an increase of 944 thousand jobs in Southern manufacturing. Of these 944 thousand jobs, 12 thousand went to Negro women and none to Negro men. The new physical capital was not to be used by Negroes.[6]

In the quality of public schools, the wide gap persisted between white and Negro schools. The official reports of the State of Mississippi continued to tell the tale. In 1961, Mississippi school boards spent, on instructional expenses, $173.42 per white student but only two thirds of that amount per Negro student.

Economic development reached the South after 1940. On farms and in cities, whites had access to the growing stock of physical capital and also to informed agricultural agents, schools, and on-the-job training which created the human capital (the Intelligence C) required to utilize the new physical capital. In contrast, Negroes were permitted limited access to accumulating capital. Whites became increasingly productive, but Negroes, denied access to machines and education, fell behind as Southern public policy widened the gap between the Intelligence C of the average white and average Negro.

C. *The North and West, 1917 to Date*

In the third time-space unit, the growing Negro population has had access to more physical capital and better education than has been available in the South. The labor shortages of the two world wars were particularly influential in bringing Negroes into Northern manufacturing activities to work with massive physical capital. In 1949, Northern Negro men enjoyed a median annual income of $2185 compared with a median of only $1033 for Southern Negro men.

The increasingly frequent recessions and rising unemployment rates of the 1950's damaged the Negro position. In 1949, Northern and Western Negro men had median incomes that were

---

[6] Alan B. Batchelder, "Poverty the Special Case of the Negro," *The American Economic Review*, May 1965, pp. 534–535.

78% as large as those of white men in those regions. In 1959, Northern and Western Negro men had median incomes that were 107% above the median income of Southern Negro men. But in 1959, the median income for Negro men in the North and West was down to 74% (from 78%) of the median income of white men in those areas. The Northern and Western Negro men were better off than their Southern peers, but were at a severe disadvantage in comparison with Northern and Western white men.[7]

One reason for this disadvantage was that almost one half of the Negroes in the Northern and Western labor force during the 1960's were born in the South where many were educated—or miseducated—in Southern schools. For most graduates of even moderately good public schools, it is extremely difficult to imagine how little education has been provided by the Southern way of life, until they meet someone "educated" on $6.67 a year.

White attitudes toward Negroes derive partly from stereotypes and partly from contact with Negro families with $6.67-a-year educations. Usually these whites will contend that, because the Negroes that they know are productively inferior, *all* Negroes must be similarly inferior. The resulting feeling of superiority induces such whites to discriminate on the basis of color rather than talent. This discrimination, in education and in employment, leads to inferior Intelligence C and greater poverty in Negroes, and these results tend to assure these whites that they were right in the first place.

On the other hand, most whites who in recent years have enrolled in the better universities of America have experienced the chastening effects of being beaten by dark-skinned competitors demonstrating unchallengeable intellectual superiority. The resulting racial attitude in the second-place whites is inevitably more respectful than that of whites sheltered from such competition. It is likely that the attitude of previously sheltered whites will change as the number of Negroes passing through good schools increases.

[7] Alan B. Batchelder, "Decline in the Relative Income of Negro Men," *The Quarterly Journal of Economics,* November 1964, p. 529.

There will be changes in the future. For the present, Negro access to economic development is restricted. White immigrants needed only Intelligence B, ambition, education, and hard work to become successes and put their children into the White House. Negroes face racial discrimination that does not bend before talent or accomplishment. Discriminatory feelings are so intense and so widespread that each Negro learns early that *regardless* of his Intelligence B, his ambition, his education, or his effort, many whites will still call him "nigger," most whites will prefer to avoid him; and few will invite him to live next door.

V. BITTER FRUITS

Many discriminatory barriers have fallen in recent years, but the effects of past and present discrimination persist not only in inferior educational attainments but also in the "blasting" suffered by Northern and Western as well as by Southern Negro families. Learning begins in the family, but discrimination has blasted the family system of poor Negroes leaving them incapable of emulating white middle-class families in preparing their children to learn the Intelligence C's valued in the American economy. Because of blasting, poor Negro families are likely to perpetuate poverty in their children. The importance of this tendency is reflected in the SSA count of children living in poor families in 1963. The SSA criteria counted 15.7% of white children but 60.0% of nonwhite children as living in poor families in 1963.

What are the symptoms of blasting? First, poor Negro families are different. Poor urban Negro families—crowded because of relatively high housing costs (10 to 25% higher than for whites in similar quarters) and many children—lack books, pencils, and a safe outdoors to explore. Adults have a small vocabulary and use it with poor diction. Women headed 23% of nonwhite families (9% of white families) in 1963. In 1862, 82% of Negro births were illegitimate. In 1962, 22% were illegitimate and many Negro babies were unwanted. Fewer Negro families would be headed by women if there were a decrease in the number of women with children they did not want. As is presently the case, 32% of poor Negro families are headed by women while in many other families women earn more than men. In most white families, masculinity means being the financial pillar of the family. Poor Negro children daily observe a different system.

Second, the Negro self-image is different. Charles Silberman observed that Negroes "learn in earliest childhood of the stigma attached to color in the United States. . . . Negroes are taught to despise themselves." [8] Asked to choose between white and brown dolls, 60% of 3-year-old Negro children pick white dolls as "the nice ones." When given an outline of a child and told to crayon it the color "you like other children to be," 37% of Negro children aged 5 to 7 choose white and 15% use a bizarre color. Asked to complete the sentence "When I look at other boys and girls, and then look at myself, I feel . . . ," 30% of white but 80% of Negro first graders of all social classes comment unfavorably about themselves (for example, "I feel ashamed").

To succeed in our economy, children must believe they can succeed, and then must work and study in pursuit of success. Lacking a belief that ambition and effort can lead to success, Negro children will not work to acquire Intelligence C. Without Intelligence C, Negro children will not succeed. They will not equal whites in the marketplace as long as they reject themselves.

Nor can Negro children succeed while their teachers reject them. And teachers do reject their Negro children, according to psychologist Kenneth Clark who spent years observing ghetto schools:

A key component of the deprivation which afflicts ghetto children is that generally their teachers do not expect them to learn . . . these children, by and large, do not learn because they are not being taught effectively and they are not being taught because those who are charged with the responsibility of teaching them do not believe that they can learn, do not expect that they can learn and do not act toward them in ways which help them to learn. [9]

---

[8] Charles E. Silberman, *Crisis in Black and White*, Random House, New York, 1964, p. 11.
[9] Kenneth B. Clark, *Dark Ghetto*, Harper and Row, New York, 1965, pp. 132 and 131.

Objective evidence supporting this charge is that the longer Negro children attend ghetto schools the more their IQ's decrease. Experiments conducted in New York, St. Louis, and Nashville schools have also supported the charge by showing that when incumbent teachers in ghetto schools are replaced by teachers who expect the children to learn, the children learn much more than under the kind of teacher attitudes that are typical in the Negro ghetto schools.

VI. DISCRIMINATION IN EMPLOYMENT

Negroes suffer discrimination before birth. They suffer discrimination in education and training. They also suffer discrimination in employment; this kind of discrimination, like the other two kinds, tends to increase the incidence of poverty among Negroes and other disadvantaged minority groups.

Rural Southern whites educated in shacks and born of mothers ill-attended during pregnancy, nevertheless have access to credit and to urban jobs that are out of reach of Negroes with similar backgrounds. In the North and West, these poorly educated whites from Southern farms are more readily accepted by employers than are poorly educated Negroes. Operating at the unskilled level as well as at the skilled and professional levels, this kind of discrimination keeps Negroes from working with physical capital in quantities that would raise their productivity and incomes above the poverty line.

Discrimination by labor unions and by employers is widespread. Some barriers have diminished in recent years. Congress has now made it illegal for larger employers to discriminate, but employment discrimination remains extensive and will continue to be so among small and large employers. It will continue to bar Negroes from merited promotions, to exclude them from jobs for which they are qualified, and to keep the unemployment rate for Negroes at double the rate for whites. Thus, discrimination will continue to raise the incidence of poverty among Negroes and other minority groups in these ways:

1. By excluding qualified individuals from work, training, or both, that would use their qualifications.

2. By discouraging youths who would otherwise train to acquire higher skills.

VII. SUMMARY

Judged by the standards of nineteenth-century America, the economic position of American Negroes is very high. But during the past 100 years, economic development has transformed the economy of white America while leaving Negroes and members of other minority groups cut off from the accumulating capital of the twentieth century.

Negroes (and the other three minorities)—discriminated against before and during birth, throughout the educational process, and in the employment market; restricted in access to physical and human capital—are in a position that few majority whites can envy. Turbulent emotions are stirred by a list of all the discriminatory factors operating to injure the minority position. However, much can be learned by forswearing value judgments and confining attention to an objective survey of the forces that operate through home, school, community, and employment office to create differences between Negroes and whites in the incidence of poverty.

PART *IV*

PROGNOSIS

9

Palliatives: Transfers from Peter to Paul

The causes of poverty analyzed in the four preceding chapters should be reviewed in light of the poverty statistics of Chapter 3. At the same time, the poor need to be divided into two groups on the basis of whether individuals can or cannot *earn* their way out of poverty. In the second group are the people least able to earn their way out of poverty—the elderly. In 1963, among the unattached individuals who were poor, 52% were 65 years of age or older. Among heads of poor families, 22% were 65 or older.

In the first group are those people who are unable to earn their way in the short run, but who are potentially able to do so in the long run. This group includes children, women heading families with children requiring their attendant care, ill-educated and ill-located adults of working age, and minority group members experiencing the effects of discrimination in education and employment. Of the 29.7 million members of poor families in 1963, one half were children under 18. Of the 7.2 million heads of poor families, 27% were women, 28% were nonwhite, 10% were farmers, and 28% worked full time for 50 or more weeks during the year.

People with more-than-poverty productivity are poor in the short run, when unable to obtain full-time, year-round work. However, in the statistics they are grouped together with the lower productivity people who cannot find full-time, year-round work. Among heads of poor families in 1963, almost

20% were unsuccessful in their efforts to obtain full-time employment.

These categories overlap repeatedly; many poor people appear in two or more of them, yet the chief causes of poverty that stand out conspicuously are: age, color, absence of a male family head, unemployment, and low productivity due to inferior education.

Among the 34.6 million poor in 1963, some could never earn their way out of poverty; others could not do so in the short run. Their only route of escape was transfer payments—gifts—from the nonpoor through either private or government channels. Others among the 1963 poor could escape poverty immediately by moving into work using their existing potential. Many others could work their way out of poverty only after accumulating more education.

This chapter describes existing transfer programs. The next chapter describes trends and current programs that raise the productivity and earning ability of the poor. These two chapters merely describe. Controversy is deferred until Chapter 11 which surveys the issues raised by the prospect of changes in transfer programs and in various other activities that affect the incidence of poverty in the United States.

I. TRANSFERS OR EARNED INCOME

The incidence of poverty in the United States is pushed up or down by a variety of events. There are many such events. However, in terms of economic function, all of them fall into one of two categories. The character of these categories and the differences between them can be demonstrated most clearly through graphic illustrations. These illustrations require the use of bars representing the respective incomes of a typical poor family and a typical nonpoor family. Each bar is drawn to a height proportional to the height of the income of that family. Poor and nonpoor families appear as in Figure 9-1.

Using these bars to distinguish the categories, we must separate the concepts of earned income and transfers. Earned income involves a quid pro quo—income is received in exchange for a person's contribution to production.

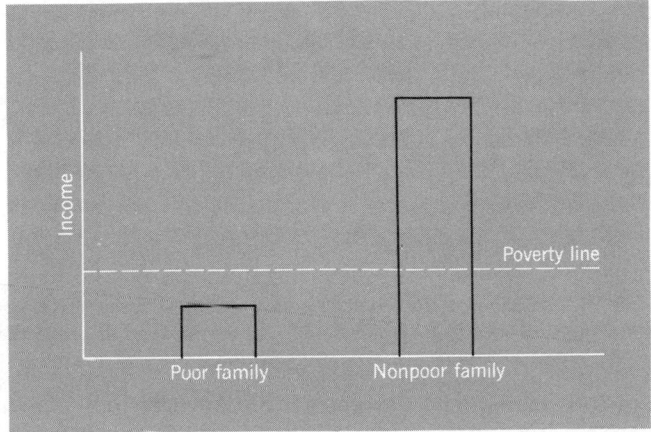

Figure 9-1. Relative incomes of typical poor and nonpoor families.

The first category of events that change the incidence of poverty consists of transfers that subtract part of the income from one column and add it to the other column. Poverty is increased if the transfer occurs from the poor to the nonpoor family as indicated in Figure 9-2. Poverty can be reduced or eliminated if the transfer occurs from the nonpoor to the poor family. This category is economically distinct because

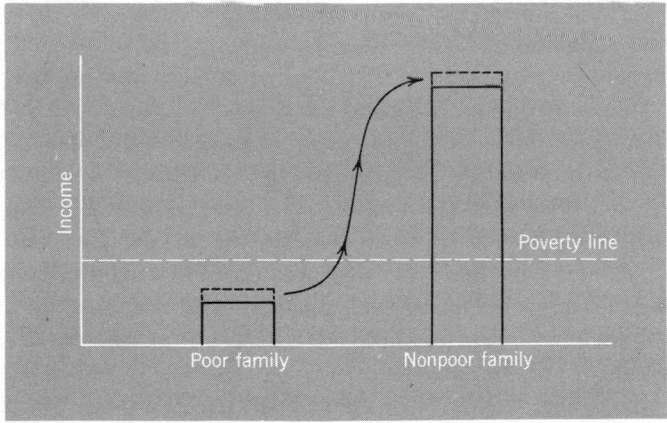

Figure 9-2. Transfers from a typical poor family to a typical nonpoor family.

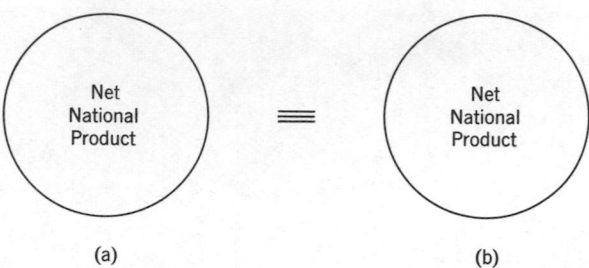

(a)   (b)

Figure 9-3. Net national product before and after transfers affecting poverty. (a) Before transfers affecting poverty. (b) After transfers affecting poverty.

the transfers changing the extent of poverty do not affect the size of total output.

Circular diagrams are used to underscore the point that transfers can change the incidence of poverty without changing the total output. This is shown in Figure 9-3.

It is convenient to assume that population size remains constant. Changes in population make the analysis arithmetically more difficult (per capita instead of total concepts must then be used), but have *no* effect on the conclusions reached. The assumption of unchanged population size eases the analysis and causes no change in the conclusions.

The second category of events affecting poverty in the United States involves changes in earned income, which represent a change in the size of net national product. NNP may be cut in physical size; this is called a contraction (as distinct from a deflation, which decreases the prices rather than the quantities of goods and services). A contraction would cause a reduction in the size of the NNP circle shown in Figure 9-3. Such a contraction can (as noted in Chapter 4) increase the incidence of poverty in a country. The reduction in size of the NNP can result either from declining demand (rising unemployment) or from reductions in individual efficiency (for example, as a result of increased discrimination).

On the other hand, NNP may grow in physical size; this is called an expansion (as distinct from an inflation, which increases prices rather than the quantities of goods and services). An expansion involves the kind of increase in NNP represented by the diagrams of Figure 9-4.

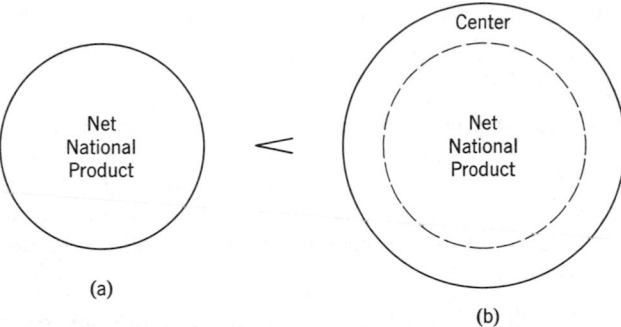

(a)

(b)

Figure 9-4. Net national product before and after expansion affecting poverty. (a) Before expansion affecting poverty. (b) After expansion affecting poverty.

An expansion can affect poverty in one of the three ways represented in Figure 9-5. Such growth in output can result either from increasing demand that reduces unemployment, from growth in quantity and quality of capital, or from reductions in the effect of market imperfections that limit productivity.

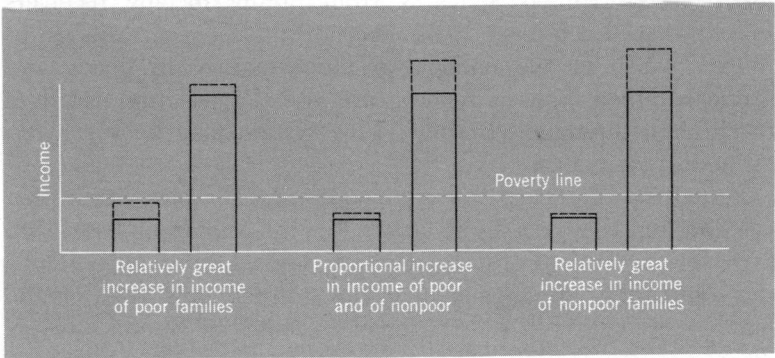

Figure 9-5. Possible effects of expansion upon the incomes of typical poor and of typical nonpoor families.

Although it is desirable to provide an *objective* analysis of events in each of the two categories, it may be appropriate to recognize the subjective ethical distinction that Western culture has traditionally made between them as means for alleviating poverty. An explicit ranking of the two categories was offered by the great scholar Moses Maimonides (1135 to 1204) who observed in *Mishneh Torah:*

There are eight degrees in the giving of charity, one higher than the other. The highest degree, than which there is nothing higher, is to take hold of a man who has been crushed and to give him a gift or a loan, or to enter into partnership with him, or to find work for him, and thus to put him on his feet so that he will not be dependent on his fellow-men.[1]

Maimonides then described seven other kinds of charity—all emphasizing transfers and all ethically lower than the first kind of charity, which was the only one of the eight that reduced poverty by increasing total output. Most Americans share this judgment that it is morally better to reduce poverty by increasing earned income rather than by increasing transfers.

II. PRIVATE TRANSFERS

Most children, left to support themselves, would perish of want. Yet, few children in the United States do perish of want. They do not perish because the biggest transfer payment in the United States is from family income receivers to children. Each year, tens—nearly hundreds—of billions of dollars worth of the national product, mostly in goods and services rather than in money, are transferred from relatives to children through the family. This system may be succinctly termed "momma-care."

Perpetuation of any society requires that some institution provide for the people—at least, for the children—unable to care for themselves. In the United States, the family fulfills this obligation. Americans take for granted this role of the family, although other arrangements could be used, such as

---

[1] Moses ben Maimon quoted in Jacob S. Minkin, *The World of Moses Maimonides,* Thomas Yoseloff, New York, 1957, p. 369.

the communal nurseries in parts of mainland China. Nevertheless, momma-care continues to be the most important kind of transfer.

Momma-care begins in infancy. Children old enough to work (age 16, 12, or 6?) do not require it, but in the United States these children, nevertheless, receive tens of billions of dollars in transfers from their families. Even college students, unquestionably old enough to produce, receive summer home care plus money for tuition, room, board—and even for convertibles—while away at college. Many, although not all, of these transfers are used to increase human capital and productivity by educating the youth; thus, current transfers reduce poverty and are designed to increase the total product later.

Momma-care transfers may go much further. In extreme cases, sons taken into family businesses or law firms live out their entire lives in the womb-like security of extended momma-care.

The institution of the family gives additional billions of dollars to elderly relatives. Some elders, like small children unable to work, would be poor without transfers. Others could work, but choose leisure instead because they are permitted to do so by family transfers.

The family aids a third group: persons rendered unproductive or of low-productivity because of physical or mental imperfection, injury, or disease. These individuals are kept from poverty by the billions of dollars worth of national product transferred to them each year by their families.

The perfectly functioning market economy of competitive private enterprise would leave in poverty millions of American youth and millions of aged and incapacitated persons. However, the institution of the family provides transfers of more than $100 billion, which keeps most, but not all, of these people out of poverty.

Poverty is also reduced when individuals and families donate to persons unrelated to them. Poor families and individuals receive gifts of food, clothing, and money from people who know them and feel able to give. If the country's 40 million nonpoor families averaged $10 worth of such gifts a year, the total annual amount would be $400 million. Is the actual figure larger or smaller? We can only guess.

The Judeo-Christian heritage is interlaced with admonitions, exhortations, and commands that the nonpoor "should" give to the poor.

> He that hath mercy on the poor, happy is he.
>
> *Proverbs 14:21*
>
> Give to the poor, and thou shalt have treasure in heaven.
>
> *Matthew 19:21*
>
> It is more blessed to give than to receive.
>
> *Acts 20:35*

Under the prodding of the National Jewish Welfare Board's associated agencies, the incidence of poverty is much lower among Jews than among gentiles. Roman Catholic agencies, such as the National Conference of Catholic Charities (a coordinating agency), the National Council of Catholic Men, The National Council of Catholic Women, the National Catholic Rural Life Conference, the Society of St. Vincent de Paul, and other groups operate with budgets of millions of dollars (not all for the poor) to reduce poverty in the United States.

In contrast, American Protestant churches transfer relatively small sums from nonpoor to poor. In 1954, a National Council of Churches survey of Protestant social welfare agencies found that most of the income of these agencies derived from fees and community chests. In 1954, the net national product was almost $337 billion. As a liberal guess based on the National Council figures, $100 million (0.0003 of 1954 net national product) was transferred by Protestant social welfare agencies from nonpoor Protestants to the poor.

Nearly every Protestant pastor has a contingency fund, part of which he uses to provide transfers to the poor. Collectively, these transfers may involve several million dollars. There were about 310 thousand Protestant churches in the United States in 1965. If the contingency-fund transfers to the poor averaged $1000 a church, the total amount would have been $310 million (0.00046 of 1965's $676 billion net national product). If the average was $100, the total was $31 million (0.000046 of the 1965 net national product). Either figure would be rivaled by the suburban building program of a single major denomination in the United States.

The Salvation Army and the Volunteers of America operate independently of other religious denominations. They spend perhaps $100 to $200 million a year, and most of this money goes to help the poor. A host of other agencies and individuals sometimes help the poor: the YWCA, YMCA, Goodwill Industries, Travelers Aid Societies, individual doctors, the Girl Scout and Boy Scout organizations, the Red Cross, fraternal lodges, service clubs, foundations, The American Cancer Society, and other health groups. Together these groups are not likely to transfer more than $1 billion to the poor.

In short, private transfers, excluding those within families, are relatively unimportant today. The point is labored here because two relevant questions are raised in the final chapter: (1) "Would government transfers be smaller if private transfers were larger?" and (2) "Would America be a better place if private transfers were larger and government transfers smaller?"

Improved transportation, urbanization, and the ignorance resulting from urban isolation have all brought on the contraction of private charity. As Chapter 4 emphasized, in the small towns of older America the poor and the nonpoor mixed together so that the nonpoor were familiar with the condition of the poor in their town or township. The nonpoor of a town knew the poor by name; the nonpoor knew where each poor family lived, how many children it had, and what its special problems were. Transfers were then made directly from nonpoor to poor and were based upon personal knowledge.

By 1960, small towns were scarce; 65% of the population lived in 212 metropolitan areas of 75 thousand or more people. Most of the 116 million people in these areas and most of the people in smaller cities commuted between places of work and residences that were set apart by income levels. Thus poor and nonpoor could not rub elbows off the job. If we were to ask a suburban husband to draw up a list of the first and last names of poor people he knows, not to mention the names or even the number of their dependents, we would probably draw a blank. There are poor Americans.

The nonpoor know of them as a mass, but they do not know them as individuals. What obligation can the suburban husband feel to people he does not know?

The behavior of Protestant churches may stem from similar causes. In middle-sized towns, Protestant churches have stratified economically—Episcopal and Presbyterian with the highest income groups, and evangelical sects with the lowest. In such churches, nonpoor meet nonpoor; poor meet poor. In big cities, each Protestant church serves the economic group of its area. In suburban churches, nonpoor Methodists meet nonpoor Methodists. In city churches poor Methodists meet poor Methodists. Similar economic segregation exists in the other denominations. In this system, most charity must be between strangers.

In contrast, most Jewish synagogues and Catholic parishes encompass wider and, therefore (usually), more diversified congregations. Poor and nonpoor meet together to worship. Charity then passes among people who meet together each Sabbath.

Outside the Jewish and Roman Catholic religious communities, the impersonalization of private transfers has culminated in the community chest and the united fund drives. In this case the recreational, educational, and medical research agencies of a community take most of the receipts but leave some money for the agencies that make transfers to the poor. Here, the splitting of the pot is decided not by the contributors but by the community fund directors. One commentator has concluded as follows:

The great changes in voluntary welfare in the twentieth century . . . have been its centralization, mechanization, and ever increasing subordination to those who are masters of its financing. No longer is the small agency serenely independent as it works for humanitarian causes entirely of its own choosing, financed by its friends. More than most Americans would care to admit, the former motivating spirit of charity and mercy has been replaced by competitive spirit, desire for progress, and obsession with efficiency—all bearing the aspect of being ends in themselves. Economic aid to individuals has been almost entirely depersonalized; the person being helped cannot even be sure that the giver intended that a person with his problem be helped. . . . The act of individual charity [has been] increasingly dehydrated by the united fund-raising technique. The contributor often feels little or no thrill as he gives to "the one big cause." On the whole, he has little sense of accomplishment as he signs a pledge form . . . to him it is likely to be almost like a tax—"just another tax". . . . Clearly, Americans are not living the kind of life in their sanitary suburbs that facilitates much contact with the world of pain and strain. We may not be enthusiastic about depersonalized giving, but few of us would have the slightest idea where to begin a new personal routine of person-to-person direct charity.[2]

III. GOVERNMENT TRANSFERS

A variety of local, state, and federal programs transfer portions of the national product to the poor. Table 9-1 shows the size of the largest of these programs and the number of beneficiaries. The table also shows how much of each program's transfers derive from federal taxes, and how much derive from local and state taxes. The total dollars involved do not, it must be emphasized, all go to the poor—especially not in the case of old-age, survivors, and disability insurance nor, to a lesser extent, in the cases of unemployment compensation or pensions to veterans and their families. The total figure of $31.2 billion goes to the noninstitutional population. The institutional poor of mental hospitals, orphanages, and prisons are not considered in this table.

These government transfers were designed in *most* cases to provide income to persons who would be poor in the perfectly functioning market economy because of old age, youth, physical or mental imperfection, injury, or disease. Noting exceptions where appropriate, we review these transfer programs within the following context.

A. *Transfers Alleviating Poverty Associated with Old Age*

1. Old-age, survivors, and disability insurance (OASDI), a program operated exclusively by the Federal Government, was begun in 1935, and is usually referred to simply as "Social Security." Initially, workers in many industries were excluded

---

[2] Vaughn Davis Bornet, *Welfare in America,* University of Oklahoma Press, Norman, 1960, pp. 139–141.

Table 9-1 Government Transfers Having Substantial Poverty-Reducing Effects: In Order of Size of 1964 Transfers (in Millions of Dollars)

	Dollar Transfers, 1964[a]			Number of Beneficiaries,
Program	State and Local	Federal	Total	December 1964
Old-age, survivors, and disability insurance		16,160	16,160	19,800,000
Pensions to veterans and their families		4,004	4,004	4,436,000
Unemployment insurance	2,663	617	3,280	1,449,000[b]
Old-age assistance	812	1,233	2,045	2,159,000
Workmen's compensation	1,605	65	1,670	
Aid to dependent children	631	1,018	1,649	4,289,000
School lunches	290	409	699	
Temporary disability insurance[c]	480		480	
Aid to the permanently and totally disabled	229	246	475	528,000
General assistance (Relief)	275		275	346,000
Medical assistance for the aged	246	202	448	227,000
Aid to the blind	52	46	98	96,000

[a] Only dollar transfers are shown; the administrative costs of the programs are excluded.
[b] Average weekly number.
[c] Four states: Rhode Island, California, New Jersey, and New York.

Source. Statistical Abstract of the United States: 1965, U. S. Government Printing Office, Washington, D.C., 1965, pp. 274, 283, 290, 300, 306, 307.

from coverage. Today, 95% of all persons in paid employment (except people employed by state and local governments with their own pension programs) work in jobs for which OASDI coverage is authorized by law. Occasionally, from year to year, Congress has expanded the program by legislating wider coverage, higher benefit payments, and higher supporting taxes. In 1965,

payments to a retired worker averaged $78.00 a month, $936.00 a year; payments to an aged widow averaged $68.50 a month, $822.00 a year; revenue came from a 7.25% tax on all of a covered worker's income below $4801; the self-employed paid 5.4% of their income below $4801.

Per capita payments were raised 7% by Congress during 1965. In 1966, payments were to rise again as Medicare took effect, and the supporting tax was to rise to 7.7% for employees and to 5.8% for the self-employed on the first $6600 of earned income. Increases up to 9.7% for employees and 7% for the self-employed are expected by 1973. OASDI also provides for widows under the age of 62, for children of deceased workers, and for disabled workers, but the primary effect is to aid the elderly, not all of whom would be poor in the absence of OASDI. Benefits were paid to 15.6 million elderly persons in 1964—74.5% of the total population aged 65 and over.

2. Old-age assistance is administered by local governments and is financed from federal, state, and local taxes. The number participating in this old-age assistance reached a peak of about 2.8 million in 1950 and has fallen 1 to 2% each year since 1950 as recipients die and as a larger and larger share of workers reaching retirement age are eligible for OASDI benefits. The amount of the population 65 years of age and over receiving OASDI benefits was 1.6% in 1940, 36.6% in 1954, and 76% in 1965. In 1965, old-age assistance payments averaged $70.50 per month, $846 a year. Because so many Negroes worked all their lives in agriculture, in services, or in casual labor when these were not covered by OASDI, Negroes are overrepresented on old-age assistance roles and underrepresented on OASDI roles. Negroes make up 11% of the population, 6.2% of persons drawing OASDI, and 38% of persons receiving old-age assistance.

3. Medical care to the aged (the Kerr-Mills program) has been administered locally and provides medical care to aged persons *not* receiving old-age assistance (and unwilling to make the state their primary heir—the legal step prerequisite to obtaining old-age assistance in most states). In 1965, 41 states participated in the program; 9 states were not participating. Benefit payments averaged $190 a month. Medicare will replace this program in the last half of the 1960's.

B. Transfers Alleviating Poverty Associated with Youth

1. Aid to Dependent Children (ADC), whose parents are absent or disabled, is administered locally. Payments vary widely among states. In 1965,

Mississippi payments averaged $9.11 a month, $109.32 a year for each child; the average for all states was $34 a month, $408 a year for each child; but ADC families averaged four children per family; so the average payment for all states was $136 a month, $1632 a year for each family.

Among ADC recipients, Negroes are overrepresented. Under slavery, Southern whites in most instances prohibited Negro marriages in order to keep individuals free for sale and to keep the Negro woman's bed open to the masters and their sons (70 to 80% of American Negroes are part white; this mixing derives from the aggressive activities of Southern white men, who—catching their breath—complain that Negro men might chase white women). In the South after 1865, change was minimized as whites kept the Negro "in his place" by keeping the Negro *man* "in his place." Southern whites lynched Negro men who dared to act like white men in speech, in business, *or* in the protection of women. Both Southern and non-Southern Negro men have been kept from "white work" (not all of them, but many) by lack of education or by employer rules excluding them. In contrast, Negro women have obtained more education and better jobs than Negro men. The result has been matriarchy within many Negro families. Marriage is a strong institution among one half of the American Negro families; marriage is weak to absent among the other half (in contrast to Brazil, where the Roman Catholic Church did not oppose but, instead, accepted and sanctified marriage of Negro slaves, and where Negro families are patriarchal today). Within the half of the Negro population where marriage is weak or absent, young Negro women—unmarried or deserted—have small children (*very* often unwanted, frequently left with female relatives) who depend upon government transfers. Negroes make up 11% of the total population; 42% of ADC recipients are Negroes.

2. OASDI payments to children of deceased workers. In 1965, 2.8 million children benefitted from these payments.

3. Payments to children of deceased veterans benefitted about 1 million children during 1965.

4. The school lunch program received federal help beginning in 1935. The avowed objects are to dispose of agricultural surpluses and to raise nutritional levels.

C. Transfers Alleviating Poverty Associated with Physical or Mental Imperfections, Injury, or Disease

1. Workmen's compensation is an insurance program required by state laws. Employers must insure either with the state or with private companies. Compensation is paid for medical expenses and for working time lost because of job-associated injuries or disease.

2. Temporary disability insurance in four states (Rhode Island was the first with such a program in 1943) provides transfers during unemployment caused by inability to work owing to any disease or accident (curiously, pregnancy makes women eligible for benefits in California and New Jersey).

3. Aid to the permanently and totally disabled, begun in 1950 as an adjunct to OASDI, is a federal program transferring income to the eligible disabled and ·their dependents. In 1965, benefits averaged $83.50 a month—$1002 a year.

4. Veterans pensions date back to the Plymouth Colony and benefit disabled veterans and their families.

5. Aid to the blind, locally administered and federally assisted since 1935, began before the First World War. Ohio passed the first pension law for the blind in 1898. In 1965, benefits averaged $86.50 a month—$1038 a year.

D. Transfers Alleviating Poverty Associated with Market Imperfections

1. Unemployment insurance is administered by the states among which benefits and eligibility requirements vary. In every

state, persons are covered only if working for an employer of four or more persons. Benefits depend upon the wage or salary level in the job last held (benefits average about 40%) and are paid for limited periods (for example, 13 weeks). Persons are ineligible unless employed for a minimum number of months before layoff. Workers on strike or fired for misconduct are also ineligible. Persons are disqualified if they fail to appear in their local employment office once a week with evidence of job hunting, or if they refuse to accept a job offer "suitable" to their experience. The program is supported by a tax that varies among employers; and the higher the employer's record of past layoffs, the higher is the tax. In 1965, payments averaged $36 a week.

2. Aid to dependent children whose parents are unable to get work was initiated by federal law in 1962. Prior to 1962, ADC could not be paid if the father lived at home and was in good health; some fathers moved out—deserted—so the family could get help; program administrators paid surprise 1:00 A.M. visits to run a bed check to see if the mothers were truly deserted. The new program was inaugurated to keep unemployed fathers at home.

E. Transfers Alleviating Poverty from Miscellaneous Causes

General assistance is the local program for helping persons found to be in need but ineligible for other programs. It is usually paid only to unemployable persons. Payments averaged $66 a month in 1965.

Of the $31.2 billion total in 1964, 78% ($24 billion) came from the Federal Government, and 22% ($7.3 billion) from state and local governments. But OASDI and veterans' payments account for 84% ($20.2 billion) of the federal transfers. Thus, aside from these two programs, most government transfers to the poor came from state and local governments.

IV. TAXES ON POOR AND NONPOOR

To the extent that the poor pay the taxes that provide the money for government transfers, the poor receive no net benefit from these transfers. What portion of their income do the poor pay in taxes? To answer this question, we must consider local and state taxes, federal excise and corporation taxes, and the most discussed tax—the federal personal income tax. Among these three categories, federal personal income taxes are least important, and "other" federal taxes are most important. Of all government tax receipts in 1965, 29% came from federal personal income taxes, 34% from state and local taxes, and 37% from "other" federal taxes.

Ohio can be used to illustrate the impact of state and local taxes. A recent study sponsored by the Ohio Council of Retail Merchants, the Ohio Farm Bureau Federation, the Ohio AFL-CIO, and the Ohio Education Association calculated tax payments by typical families in particular income groups. These calculations disclosed that the typical family paid in state and local taxes (property, sales, city income, gasoline, unemployment compensation, and 10 others) the amounts listed in Table 9-2, shown as a percentage of income for each income group. The percentage of income paid in taxes is lower when

Table 9-2

If Family Income Was:	Then Tax Paid Was, as a Percentage of Income:
Under $2000	18.2
$3000 to $3999	11.6
$5000 to $7499	8.6
Over $9999	6.3

Source. George W. Thatcher, *Tax Revision Alternatives for the Tax System of Ohio*, Ohio Tax Study Committee, Columbus, 1962, p. 75.

income is higher because low-income families pay a higher percentage of income for housing (subject to property tax) than high-income families do. The percentage is higher also because low-income families have little insurance or savings, whereas high-income families direct part of their income into insurance and savings which are untouched by sales taxes.

Federal estate, gift, corporate profits, excise, customs, *and* social insurance taxes were estimated in the mid-1950's to have the impact shown in Table 9-3 upon typical families in each of the four income groups listed in Table 9-2.

Table 9-3

If Family Income Was:	Then Tax Paid Was, as a Percentage of Income:
Under $2000	12.6
$3000 to $3999	12.0
$5000 to $7499	10.7
Over $9999	18.6

Source. Richard A. Musgrave, "The Incidence of the Tax Structure," *Federal Tax Policy for Economic Growth and Stability,* Joint Committee on the Economic Report, 84th, 1st, Government Printing Office, Washington, D.C., November 9, 1955, p. 98.

New Social Security taxes have raised the percentage paid by low-income families more than the percentage paid by high-income families because that tax now touches only the first $6600 in income.

The federal personal income tax charges everyone exactly the same 14% on their first $500 in taxable income and exactly the same 14.5% on their second $500, and so on, for added increments of income. The rates are the same for rich and poor on any given increment, but high-income families have increments (taxed at higher rates) that low-income families do not share. Before the 1964 tax cuts, the impact of the federal personal income tax was that shown in Table 9-4.

Table 9-4

If Family Income Was:	Then Tax Paid Was, as a Percentage of Income:
Under $2000	3.4
$3000 to $3999	9.4
$5000 to $7499	10.0
Over $9999	14.0

Source. Richard Goode, *The Individual Income Tax,* The Brookings Institution, Washington, D.C., 1964, p. 326.

The percentage actually paid did not rise faster with higher incomes because people with high incomes could afford to buy information permitting them to avoid high tax rates (for example, if a family's annual income of 1 million came entirely from public school bonds, the family would pay no federal income tax).

If the Ohio figures on state and local taxes are combined with the figures on federal taxes, we can estimate their total impact on families in the particular income groups (Table 9-5).

Table 9-5

If Family Income Was:	Then Tax Paid Was, as a Percentage of Income:
Under $2000	34.2
$3000 to $3999	33.0
$5000 to $7499	29.3
Over $9999	38.9

Source. Tables 9-2, 9-3, and 9-4 above.

Do American taxes redistribute income from nonpoor to poor? In Ohio, as in most states, property and sales taxes are so high that poor and nonpoor pay about the same portion of their income in taxes. These tax receipts then finance welfare payments to raise the income of the poor. Thus, both poor and nonpoor pay out much of their income in taxes, and part of the welfare payments to the poor are financed by money taken from them. The rest of the welfare payments are financed by tax money taken from the nonpoor as governments redistribute some income from nonpoor to poor.

V. THE INCOME GAP

Surely tens of millions more Americans than are now poor would be poor if there were no private or government transfers. The $100-plus billions in private transfers and the tens of billions in government transfers shift part of each year's output from the productively nonpoor to those people whom the market would leave poor. These transfers reduce the amount of poverty in the United States but do not eliminate it.

The SSA criteria counted 34.6 million persons who, after all transfers, were still poor. The SSA then calculated the minimal dollar income that would have placed these 34.6 million people just above the poverty line; this figure was $28.8 billion in

1963. This was $11.5 billion more than the $17.3 billion received by the poor in 1963.

Where did the $17.3 billion come from? About $4.7 billion came in transfers from old-age assistance, aid to dependent children, medical aid to the elderly, aid to the permanently and totally disabled, and aid to the blind. Included in the other $12.6 billion were portions of OASDI, veterans' pensions, unemployment compensation, and other government transfers. Altogether, more than one half of the total income of the poor comes from government transfers. There are about 3 million families and unattached individuals who receive government transfers that help to keep them out of poverty; 15 to 16 million of the poor benefit from government transfers that alleviate but do not prevent poverty; and "about half of the poor now receive no public transfer income." [3]

Additional transfers of $11.5 billion (requiring an increase of 8 to 9% in the 1963 taxes of the nonpoor four fifths of the population) could have wiped out poverty in America in 1963. Some of the poor can escape poverty only by receiving bigger transfers—private or public. *But transfers can increase the income of the poor only by subtracting from the income of the nonpoor.*

The alternative means of reducing poverty is by increasing the productivity of the poor to expand national output so that the income of the poor can increase while the income of the nonpoor remains unchanged or also increases. By this means, the potentially productive poor can forego all transfers and still escape poverty. The next chapter surveys trends and existing programs that will reduce poverty by increasing the productivity of the poor and, thereby, the national output.

VI. SUMMARY

Age, color, lack of a male family head, unemployment, and lack of education are the principal causes of poverty. In the

---

[3] Council of Economic Advisers, *The Annual Report of the Council of Economic Advisers: 1966*, U. S. Government Printing Office, Washington, D.C., 1966, p. 114.

United States, the family provides the transfers that keep most of its young, aged, and infirm out of poverty. Private charity prevents or alleviates poverty in many cases, but private charity has become less and less important as the nonpoor have increasingly isolated themselves from the poor. Government transfer programs (the activities of the welfare state, expanded since the 1930's) now move between $30 and $40 billion a year. Since the incidence of taxes falls almost as heavily upon the poor as upon the nonpoor—the federal personal income tax is an exception to the general rule—welfare state transfers to the poor represent a net gain well below the gross. This is because government tax collections absorb one third of the income of poor families, and part of those collections are used to finance the transfers. More than one half of the total income of the poor comes from government transfers, but only one half of the poor benefitted from government transfers in 1965.

10

Reducing Poverty through Increases in Per Capita, Net National Product

The size of a nation's net national product depends upon the quantity and quality of its resources and the portion of them in use. Output per person depends, in turn, on two factors: size of NNP and size of population. Individual output can be increased through more complete and more efficient utilization of existing resources; by increasing the total supply of resources (by adding to technical knowledge, physical capital, or human capital); or by reducing the number of persons sharing the national product.

This chapter surveys the devices through which per capita output is likely to increase in the late 1960's. Each device is considered within the context of the question: "What is its likely effect upon the poor?"

I. INCREASING PER CAPITA PRODUCT, USING EXISTING RESOURCES

A. Aggregate Demand

In March 1961, when the recession which had begun in 1960 began to ebb, 6.9% of the civilian labor force was unemployed, 5% worked short hours (although desiring full-time), and only 78% of factory capacity was utilized. By 1966, unemployment was down to 4% (a drop of more than one third), short-hour work for persons seeking full-time employment was down to 3.9% (a drop of more than one fifth), and factories were running at 91% of capacity (a rise of 13 percentage points). Thus, workers and factories that were idle in early 1961 were put to work by 1966, and those people employed only part-time in early 1961 were put to work full-time by 1966 because aggregate demand rose during the intervening 5 years.

Between the first quarter of 1961 and the last quarter of 1965, production of residential structures rose 5% a year. Federal purchases of goods and services increased 5% a year (national defense spending *fell* persistently from 1962 until July of 1965), personal consumption expenditures increased 6% a year, state and local purchases of goods and services 8%, and private business fixed investment 10%. Behind the increases in these component parts of aggregate demand were expansive monetary and fiscal policies. Monetary policy permitted the quantity of money to rise at a rate 2 to 3 *times* the rate of increase permitted during the relatively depressed years of the late 1950's. An expansive federal fiscal policy began in 1962 with depreciation reform and an investment tax credit. The Revenue Act of 1964 cut personal and corporation income tax rates enough to increase consumption and investment spending by $30 billion a year in 1965. Reductions in federal excise taxes and the liberalization of Social Security benefits more than offset the normal growth of federal revenues and provided an additional fiscal stimulus during 1965.

How has this peacetime expansion affected the poor? Between 1960 and 1964, the incidence of poverty among Americans fell almost *one fifth*, from 22.3% to 18% of the total population.[1]

The 1965 figures were sure to show a further decline. The unemployed poor and the underemployed poor of 1961 moved away from poverty as aggregate demand rose and provided additional work and additional income.

Defense spending, after declining between 1962 and 1965, rose a bit in late 1965 and continued to grow moderately during 1966. But it is more important to note that the growth of civilian

---

[1] These figures are based on the SSA criteria of Chapter 3 *except* that 70% lines have been used for farm families. Poverty-income lines were adjusted to take account of price changes between 1960 and 1964.

demand that had *by itself* supported the 1961 to 1965 expansion appeared likely to persist. This growing civilian demand, fueled by expansive monetary and fiscal policies, appeared capable of holding unemployment rates below 4%, while military needs could push the unemployment rate still lower. The employable poor, given either of these conditions, would retain access to expanding opportunities to work their way out of poverty.

B. *State Employment Offices*

Ignorance of the job market and obstacles to geographic movement prevent workers from moving into jobs that would maximize their productive efficiency. Consequently, some workers are left poor. Improvement in knowledge of employment opportunities and reductions in the obstacles to geographic movement help some poor to work their way out of poverty, even when aggregate demand stagnates. Year-to-year improvements in American education furnish better information regarding employment and investment opportunities, and some of the poor benefit from this knowledge by moving into jobs that they would not have reached without the information.

Private and government employment agencies exist as alternatives to the buddy system in bringing job hunters and vacancies together. In 1961, about 4% of all job placements occurred through fee-charging private agencies, and about 16% through state employment agencies. The state employment offices are administered entirely by the states but are financed exclusively by the Federal Government. These employment offices were begun in 1933 as part of the New Deal program to get the unemployed back to work. Their initial primary responsibility was to channel workers into the New Deal public works and relief programs. When unemployment insurance became operative in 1937, the unemployment insurance system was integrated administratively with the state employment offices. The image soon emerged that the combined agencies were *unemployment* offices.

This view seemed to extend to the staff as well as to the customers. In 1958, Secretary of Labor James P. Mitchell, at the annual meeting of the directors of the state employment offices, attacked the state employment system for a preoccupation with unemployment insurance duties that reduced the effectiveness of the system in moving unemployed workers into jobs.

This situation changed during the 1960's. The employment service has: (1) increased the percentage of applicants interviewed and tested in order to measure the productive potential of individuals; (2) moved unemployment-compensation claims offices into buildings separate from those housing the employment service offices; (3) doubled counseling and placement work with high school seniors; and (4) made more aggressive efforts to induce companies to list job openings with it.

Because so many poor are ill-informed about employment opportunities, more aggressive placement efforts by the state employment offices can be expected to move more poor people into jobs in which they will be more productive. Because so many of them are ill-informed as to their own productive potential, greater use of interviews and aptitude tests can be expected to move some poor into "antipoverty" education-training programs (discussed below) that will raise their productivity and put them into jobs and out of poverty. Will many poor be involved? That is up to the local employment offices.

C. Geographic Movement

The poor may also benefit from a reduction in obstacles to geographic movement to the best paying jobs. Many poor people remain in areas where there is no work capable of yielding them above-poverty incomes. Some remain because personal handicaps such as age, keep them from moving to better jobs. Others stay because they are ignorant of work opportunities elsewhere or because, although aware of other opportunities, they are unwilling or are financially unable to move.

The automobile has made a difference by permitting workers to move more freely to jobs offering the highest pay. Some government programs have also made a small difference. Since 1952, the Bureau of Indian Affairs has been paying the expenses of Indian families moving from the poverty of reservations to work in cities. Each year since 1952, about 5 to 6 thousand families have made the move—but 40% of these have later returned to the reservation.

In the early 1960's, several bills were introduced in Congress proposing the use of federal money to help move the able-bodied poor and their families from depressed areas to places where the family heads could get work. These bills were defeated by elected officials reluctant to lose voters in their districts and by merchants reluctant to lose customers—even customers on relief. Then, in 1963, Congress passed a law authorizing the use of federal money for grants or loans to cover the expenses of unemployed workers moving their families out of areas with high rates of unemployment and into areas where the men could get work. The program, thus far, has been small and experimental. About 2000 workers and their families have been assisted in moves out of Appalachia, northern Minnesota, and the Missouri Ozarks. The program is being continued on an experimental basis.

Other modest programs have attempted to move the poor to places where jobs will permit them to become nonpoor. The Federal Government has moved Cuban refugees, and the Ford Foundation has helped some Negroes to move from rural to urban North Carolina.

Private corporations, not curing but preventing poverty, have increasingly arranged to move employees when the companies shift location. These arrangements may not increase total employment, since 100 men who have moved take jobs that could be filled by 100 men hired at the new location. Still, the net effect might be a reduction in overall unemployment because business moves are usually from areas of economic decline to areas of economic expansion. The 100 men who might be left behind are, as a rule, less likely to find alternative work than the 100 men in the expanding area to which the company moves.

At present, corporation programs and government programs are relocating people by the thousands. Moves by individuals without such assistance take about 800 thousand persons off farms and about 6.5 million people across state lines each year. Although the majority of the migrants are not poor, some are. Most of the people moved by government and many moving independently become more productive. They also increase the size of national output, and leave poverty by moving out of poor regions.

D. *Bringing in Industry*

In 1961, the Area Redevelopment Administration was created with an annual budget of about $125 million to be used to increase private employment in areas of chronic high unemployment. The ARA could make low-interest loans to the following: (1) plants locating in a depressed area, (2) plants in a depressed area that were planning an expansion there, and (3) depressed-area governments for public facilities needed by employers. The ARA also provided technical assistance to communities planning means to expand local employment. In 1962, the Accelerated Public Works Program was authorized to distribute $900 million in federal grants to state and local governments in order to pay 50 to 75% of the cost of public facilities in depressed areas with a potential for economic growth.

In 1965, $1.1 billion was authorized by Congress to aid Appalachia, the mountainous area between central southern New York and central Alabama. Public works and other poverty-reducing projects in areas of "significant potential for future economic growth" were to receive $270 million. These areas of "significant potential" were to be identified by an Appalachian Regional Commission. Of the $1.1 billion total, $840 million (76%) were for roads that might be used by tourists and new industry coming in—or, especially if much of the remaining $270 million helped education, by the present Appalachian residents when moving out. Outmigration has been large. Between 1950 and 1960, the 190 counties of southern Appalachia lost about 1.1 million persons, (20% of their population). This rate of outmigration has continued into the 1960's. Another 20 to 30 years of such movement, and only a few poor families will remain in Appalachia.

In short, government money is used in three ways to increase production and reduce poverty by bringing unemployed workers and job vacancies together: (1) to attract industry to depressed areas; (2) to help the unemployed leave depressed areas; and (3) to provide the unemployed with more knowledge about their own potential and about existing job opportunities. This government money supplements the effects of private initiative operating in the same ways.

E. Discrimination

Discrimination keeps trained Negroes in poverty when their applications for work are rejected because they are Negroes. But this effect of prejudice is sharply reduced when aggregate demand presses unemployment rates below 4% of the labor force. The salutary effect of aggregate demand was shown during the Second World War when 1.5% unemployment rates brought Negroes into hundreds of thousands of semiskilled manufacturing jobs from which they had previously been excluded. This change was helped by white public opinion that the Nazis' Aryan racism was little different from the racism that kept Negroes out of the better occupations. But even without public reaction to racism, the high aggregate demand of the war years would have placed great pressure on white employers to hire on the basis of ability rather than race.

Since 1945, unemployment rates have never fallen below 2.9%; between 1953 and 1964, they never fell below 4.9% of the civilian labor force. This relatively weak aggregate demand left unemployment rates for whites at relatively high levels and, for Negroes, at about *double* the rate for whites. The trend since early 1961 has been toward less unemployment. This trend, if carried far enough, can greatly reduce the poverty-creating effects of racial discrimination in employment.

Statutory prohibition of racial discrimination in employment went into effect in New Jersey and New York in 1945 and in 22 other states and dozens of municipalities over the next 19 years. In July 1965, the Federal Equal Employment Opportunity Commission came into being to mediate *but not to prosecute*. Aggrieved individuals received the right to seek injunctions halting discrimination, and the United States Department of Justice received authority to prosecute large companies (100 or more employees), large unions (100 or more members), and employment agencies for denying work or membership to persons who were qualified but who were rejected on the basis of race, color, or national origin. Although the threat of government intervention hangs over many employers, governments act in only a few hundred cases a year. Thus, legislative prohibition is much less pervasive than high aggregate demand in reducing discrimination in hiring and in promotion.

In addition to government action, reduction of white prejudice is also having an effect in curbing poverty. During the 1960's, the Protestant and Catholic churches became more active advocates of judging men on the basis of performance rather than on the basis of color. Racial prejudice has been ebbing in American whites since the 1930's. Religious leaders, political leaders, and newspapers feel free to help by admonishing, "Judge by performance not color," and laws have been passed. Yet white prejudice remained effective enough in 1965 so that gross national product was $5 billion less than it would have been if unemployment rates had been as low for Negroes as for whites; gross national product could have been an additional $22 billion higher if Negroes had received as much education and training as whites by 1965.

Whether reduced discrimination will permit the $27 billion increase in gross national product during the years ahead will depend upon white prejudice and the forces operating to overcome it. Since 30% of the poor are Negroes, the extent of white racial prejudice is of primary importance in determining any change in the incidence of poverty in America.

F. *Bringing Mothers into the Labor Force*

The Federal Economic Opportunity Act of 1964 provided funds to urban areas for day-care centers so that mothers of preschool children can go to work after leaving their children where they will be well fed and well cared for. Since 35% of all poor families headed by a woman have children under age 6 (about 700 thousand poor families headed by a woman have children under age 6), these centers may help many families to escape poverty by an alternative means to higher Aid to Dependent Children.

In sum, poverty would be alleviated through more complete and more effective use of existing resources if workers were moved into more productive jobs, if the unemployment of men and machines were reduced, and if a greater number of mothers were able to enter the labor force. By employing these resources more efficiently, poverty would be reduced and the total national product would be increased. However, poverty can also be reduced when birth control holds down the number of persons sharing the output.

II. BIRTH CONTROL TO LIFT PER CAPITA SHARES

In 1960, the nonpoor could, if they wished, buy birth control information from their family doctors. But the poor who patronized only county or city welfare hospitals were denied access to all birth control information except that available in the mixture of superstition and fact known to their uneducated fellow poor. Solid Roman Catholic and occasional Protestant pressure prohibited public health agencies from providing birth control information—even when clients requested help.

During the 1960's, change occurred at the local, state, and federal levels. In 1964, there were 470 public birth control clinics in 11 states. In 1965, there were 689 (a 45% increase in 12 months) in 21 states. During 1965, the California Board of Public Health urged every California county to set up public birth control programs. Detroit and Baltimore, both with large voting Roman Catholic populations, set up local birth control clinics. In 1961, a Planned Parenthood Group began to disseminate birth control information and devices to poor families in Corpus Christi, Texas. By 1964, the group was serving about 2000 women; charity births at the city hospital were down 24%; and there was "a 40% drop-off in the number of women seeking medical treatment for incompetently performed criminal abortions." [2] President Johnson, in his 1965 State of the Union Message, warned of the population explosion. He urged, in general terms, federal assistance for programs to limit population growth, and then he specifically asked for more money for the District of Columbia birth-control clinics. During 1965, federally financed birth-control clinics were opened in Corpus Christi and a dozen other cities. The few dollars of Margaret Sanger's Planned Parenthood Foundation are now being augmented by government millions in a campaign to reduce the number of unwanted children who can push the near-poor into poverty and the already-poor into still deeper poverty.

Of the 15 million children being raised in poverty in 1963, 6.5 million (or 43%) lived in a home with at least 5 children under the age of 18. (The poverty line for a family of 6 was $2500 for a farm family; $4135 for a nonfarm family.) Of all families with 6 or more children in 1963, one half were labeled poor by the SSA criteria. Reduction in the number of unwanted children in America will bring a parallel reduction in the amount of poverty.

---

[2] Ray Shaw, "Birth Control Program Makes Early Gains in Heavily Catholic Area," *Wall Street Journal*, October 11, 1965, p. 1.

III. INCREASING THE QUANTITY OF RESOURCES

Technology—the accumulation of the knowledge of how to produce—is considered here as a resource. However, it differs from other resources in that it provides the rules for their use. Earlier chapters called attention to how technological change has reduced poverty over the centuries. Tiresome as is the cliché, "The past century has brought spectacularly unprecedented technological change," nevertheless, it is true. It is important because it leads to questions that are fundamental: What is happening to technological change in the present? What is in prospect for the future? What is the likely effect of prospective technological change upon poverty?

One measure of technological change is the number of patents granted by the United States Patent Office. Not all patents revolutionize production. Many, perhaps most, are for minor changes; some are mere gimcracks. Yet, we may assume that the portion of significant technological change that is represented in the figures remains about the same from year to year. It follows that increases in the number of significant new patents are proportionate to increases in the number of total new patents.

Table 10-1 Number of Patents Issued: Selected Years 1880 to 1964

Year	Patents Issued
1880	12,903
1920	37,060
1950	43,040
1961	48,368
1962	55,691
1963	45,679
1964	47,376

Source. U.S. Department of Commerce, *Historical Statistics of the United States,* U.S. Government Printing Office, Washington, D.C., 1960, p. 607, and *Statistical Abstract of the United States: 1965,* U.S. Government Printing Office, Washington, D.C., 1965, p. 552.

Table 10-1 shows the number of new patents issued by the United States Patent Office during selected years. The number of new patents issued during 1950 was 16% more than in 1920; the number issued during 1964 was 10% more than in 1950.

The term "production" refers to total output, whereas the term "productivity" refers to output per man-hour. Improvements in technology will continue to increase American productivity. Productivity will also be increased by additions to the stock of physical capital per person.

A. *Physical Capital per Person*

Additions to physical capital must be distinguished from improvements in technology. Using tractors as an example, an improvement in technology means construction of a new and improved tractor to *replace* an old, worn out one. An increase in physical capital means construction of *additional* tractors just like the old ones. The construction of additional tractors of improved quality would represent both improved technology *and* added physical capital (in Chapter 7, Seth and Abel improved technology *and* added physical capital).

As noted in Chapter 5, a nation that consumes everything that it produces in a year adds nothing to its stock of physical capital. A nation that consumes less than it produces, allowing for replacement of depreciation, will add to its physical capital; and if the physical capital grows more rapidly than the labor force, productivity will also increase.

Table 10-2 Reproducible Tangible Assets Valued in 1947 to 1949 Prices[a]

Year	Total (Billions)	Per Capita
1920	$ 440	$4100
1945	622	4400
1950	762	5000
1955	928	5600
1958	1022	6000

[a] Includes producers' and consumers' durables, public and private buildings, and inventories.

Source. U.S. Department of Commerce, *Statistical Abstract of the United States: 1964*, U.S. Government Printing Office, Washington, D.C., 1964, p. 347.

The United States has been adding to physical capital faster than to population and labor force. Table 10-2 shows the recent growth of America's "reproducible tangible assets." These include producers' durables (tools and machinery), consumers' durables (appliances, tools, cars), inventories, and residential, governmental, commercial, manufacturing, and farm buildings. These asset figures have all been valued in 1948 prices. The figures in the table are shown both in total and on a per capita basis for the only 5 years for which calculations have been made. Between 1920 and 1958, the per capita figure rose nearly 50%.

If consumer durables and government buildings are omitted from consideration, and if allowance is made for the replacement of $57 billion in depreciation each year, American physical capital has been rising by $40 billion a year during the mid-1960's. This is an addition *each* year of $206 worth of private buildings, inventories, and machinery for every American.

Table 10-3 Indexes of National Productivity in the Private Sector: Selected Years 1889 to 1965 (1929 = 100)

Year	Real Product per Man-hour		
	Total Economy	Farm	Nonfarm
1889	43.6	77.0	41.1
1909	65.6	88.1	64.7
1929	100.0	100.0	100.0
1937	114.0	106.8	116.4
1948	156.7	161.3	149.5
1957	211.7	265.6	192.3
1965	274.0	409.0	242.0
1970	?	?	?

Source. U.S. Department of Commerce, *Historical Statistics of the United States*, U.S. Government Printing Office, Washington, D.C., 1960, p. 559; *President's Economic Report: 1966*, U.S. Government Printing Office, Washington, D.C., 1966, p. 245.

Improved technology and accumulating physical capital have contributed to the growth of American labor productivity shown by Table 10-3. The effects of price changes have been totally excluded from the figures so that the table presents a measure of *real* output per man-hour of work in American private business. This measure rises when technology is improved and when the stock of physical capital per worker increases (and when human capital increases—we shall discuss that later). Between 1889 and

1929, (a 40-year interval), farm productivity per man-hour rose a little less than one third while nonfarm productivity more than doubled. Since 1929, nonfarm productivity per man-hour has more than doubled again, while agricultural productivity has more than quadrupled. These are the changes that raise the per capita share of output and lower the incidence of poverty.

How long can these rates of increase go on? To a greater or lesser extent, there is ingrained in every American the Puritan conviction that it is sinful to have too many material possessions. Do nonpoor Americans already have too many material possessions? Irrespective of the answer, the nonpoor are going to have *more* because more is a consequence of ingenuity, capital accumulation, and rising aggregate demand; and there is no sign of any slowdown.

Accumulated physical capital and changing technology can make even the lame, the blind, and the illiterate so productive that they become nonpoor. Surely, all American farmers would still be poor if accumulated capital and improved technology had not placed in their hands hybrid seeds, chemical fertilizers, tractors, steel plows, and all the other implements of modern agriculture, along with the knowledge of how to use them. If physical capital and technology accumulate sufficiently in the future, machines will appear that can be operated by anyone, who *with this equipment*, will be so productive as to move out of poverty by using it to increase the national product.

Improved technology and the growth of *physical* capital will increase human productivity even though the individual remains unchanged. A productive—and complicated—machine can be made to be operated by an illiterate; this has been done extensively in the United States steel industry. But it is easier to design a complex machine to be run by a high school graduate than to design one to be run by an illiterate person, and present engineering efforts concentrate on machines for the high school graduate. Thus, individuals who participate in the growth of *human* capital can now quickly convert newly acquired skill into added output and added income. Table 10-3 showed that between 1929 and 1957 American productivity more than doubled; 60% of this increase could be attributed to improved technology and accumulated physical capital; the other 40% of the increase resulted from improved education,[3] which by definition is an increase in human capital. Presumably, the 40% role of human capital continued into the 1960's.

B. Increase in Human Capital: The Home

The first grade—sometimes kindergarten, sometimes nursery school—marks the beginning of what is called formal education, but an individual's education begins at birth. By the time a child is six, he can be so miseducated as to be unlikely ever to benefit from formal schooling. If he is taught to hate school, to be indifferent, or to be totally frightened, he is unlikely to gain much from school attendance.

Most American education occurs in the home and with peers. This portion of education tends to teach the child to be like the people he knows. For the children of the poor, this means learning to behave in ways likelier to keep them poor than in the ways taught by the example of suburban white, Protestant, Anglo-Saxon, certified-public-accountant fathers.

Much is being done with the poor to bend the twigs the other way. Given the state of technology and the amount of physical capital in any year, the poor individual of low productivity can move out of poverty if he has the Intelligence B required and the access to training that will permit him to work his way out of poverty by increasing his productivity. This is the potential that education offers both the children of the poor *and* the adult poor.

C. Increase in Human Capital: Public Schools

The chief instrument of formal education in the United States is the public school system, supplemented by parochial and other private schools. These public and nonpublic schools, in addition to making life more fun, build the human capital required to run the American economy efficiently. Free public schools are available to all American children, except in Mississippi where children are denied free admission to public schools if their parents are dead or live in another state. In Mississippi, these

---

[3] E. F. Denison, *The Sources of Economic Growth in the United States*, Committee for Economic Development, New York, 1962, p. 73.

children can go to school only if someone is willing—and able—
to pay tuition for them. With the exception of Mississippi, the
American school system is *the* agency likeliest to provide the
means by which the children of the poor can escape the poverty
of their parents.

In 1964, $39 billion was spent on public and nonpublic schools
—kindergarten through graduate and professional schools. This
was 6.8% of the net national product. Most of this 6.8% went to
the children of the nonpoor; some went to the poor—but only
to those who were in school. Of children aged 6 to 15 in 1964,
98.8% were in school. Of youths aged 16 to 17, 87.7% were in
school; the 12.3% who were not in school were mostly the
children of the poor. By dropping out, these youths were well
on the way to remaining in poverty.

The 6.8% of the net national product went to children in school,
but was not equally divided among them. School board members
usually come from nonpoor neighborhoods and represent the
interests of the middle class. They are primarily concerned with
the education of their children, the boys and girls bound for
college. School boards (North, South, and West), provide better
buildings, better teachers, better equipment, greater course
variety and, of course, more money per pupil to schools in nonpoor neighborhoods than to schools in poor neighborhoods. In
the South, this differential was increased by the system of forced
segregation in which "separate but equal" was always—and
everywhere—known to be a euphemism for "separate and *very*
unequal."

There is now a trend toward more equal division of school funds
among pupils. The chief force pressing in this direction is
federal aid to education. In recent years, many governors have
been elected on a platform of "No new taxes." As school expenses rise, these governors and their supporters are gradually
pulling their state governments out of public education. The
gap is being filled by the Federal Government which in 1951,
paid for about 1% of public school costs and, in 1966, absorbed
10% of these costs.

Congressional emphasis differs somewhat from that of most
school boards. When Congress passed legislation in 1965 providing federal aid to elementary and secondary schools, it

"declared it the policy of the United States to provide financial assistance to local education agencies serving areas with concentrations of children from low income families." [4] Congress then appropriated $967 million of which $775 million was to go to "educationally deprived children." In practice, the $775 million was to be divided among school districts in proportion to the number of children aged 5 to 15 from families with incomes under $2000 a year (*net* of any relief receipts). Congress seems to have committed itself to helping poor children to catch up with nonpoor children of equal Intelligence B who are ahead because superior homes and neighborhoods have helped them learn to be productive.

D. *Increase in Human Capital: Adult Training and Education*

Elementary and secondary schools provide the principal instruments aiding the children of the poor to escape poverty. But a variety of programs for adult training and education offer access to higher productivity for those who prefer to learn with their hands rather than with their heads, who missed out when first in school, or who have been stranded by technological displacement. Table 10-4 gives selected statistics for these programs.

Formal on-the-job training (OJT) is available and is utilized by 3% of the employed civilian labor force during a period of high and rising employment. The impact of OJT on the poor, who need it most, depends upon the level of aggregate demand. If aggregate demand is low (unemployment high), OJT is minimal; employers, if hiring at all, are able to hire experienced workers for all but the newest kinds of jobs. When aggregate demand is high (and unemployment low), employers seeking labor and faced with inexperienced workers pursue two tacks:

1. Jobs are adapted (meaning simplified to suit the available workers.

2. Inexperienced workers receive OJT to learn how to handle the work.

Employers unhappily refer to this situation as "scraping the bottom of the labor barrel," but they successfully assume the

---

[4] *Congressional Quarterly Weekly Report*, 2 April 1965, p. 574.

Table 10-4 Enrollment in Adult Education and Training Programs

Kind of Program	Number Enrolled	Year to which Enrollment Figures Apply
On-the-job training	2,500,000	1962
Apprentices	85,000	1960
Adult education in high schools	3,421,000	1958-1959
Military vocational training	⅔ of new personnel	
Area Redevelopment Administration	12,786	1964
Manpower Development and Training	229,380	1964

Source. Sar Levitan, Federal Manpower Policies and Programs to Combat Unemployment, The Upjohn Institute, Kalamazoo, 1964, p. 24; U.S. Department of Health, Education and Welfare, Digest of Educational Statistics: 1965, U.S. Government Printing Office, Washington, D.C., 1965, p. 28; Manpower Report of the President, 1965, U.S. Government Printing Office, Washington, D.C., 1965, pp. 251–254.

burdens caused by a market so attractive that it justifies the inconvenience of adapting both inexperienced workers and complex jobs so that they fit together. The most spectacular success of employers in this area occurred during the Second World War when millions of women, previously unable to fasten a nut on a bolt, were put to work as welders, riveters, and assemblers of guns, tanks, and airplanes. The assembly of *air-planes,* a highly technical task in 1940, was adapted to adaptable women in 1942. OJT raises the productivity and income of tens of thousands of the poor when aggregate demand justifies the expense to employers of running such a program.

Apprenticeship is a separate category of OJT. In 1950, there were 110 thousand apprentices; in 1960, there were only 85 thousand. Most apprenticeship programs are run as instruments of monopoly power by unions that admit only sons or nephews of incumbents, while seeking to restrict the supply and hold up the price of their service. Apprenticeship rarely helps the poor; apprenticeship restrictions raise the prices of the things the poor buy.

The United States Department of Defense spends hundreds of millions of dollars each year to train hundreds of thousands of servicemen in occupations that they will pursue after being discharged to civilian life. Many of these men were poor when sworn into military service but are able to work their way out of poverty after discharge.[5] Yet, during the 1960's, 50% of all draftees have been rejected: 24% have been medically disqualified; 22% have failed the mental test (48.3% in Mississippi) and 3% have both failed the mental test and been disqualified medically (8% in Mississippi). Many of these flunkouts were poor. Thus, the military trains many poor, but has admissions criteria that exclude from military schools the men most in need of training. Since early 1964, these rejects have been offered special training and counseling through the state employment service.

For decades, state and local governments have aided the poor through public schools financed by transfers and through assistance payments. During the 1930's, the Federal Government began participating in the assistance payment programs with a split between federal and state-local financing, which was described in Chapter 9. Federal assistance to public schools began in 1918 with almost $1.7 million from the Smith-Hughes Act (mostly for agriculture education). Since 1960, the Federal Government has initiated new programs to aid the poor *not* by assistance payments but through education for both older juveniles *and* adults. The first of these innovations was the Area Redevelopment Administration (ARA) program for unemployed workers in depressed areas. The ARA provided training for up to 16 weeks for the unemployed unskilled and for persons who were unable to find jobs using their old skills (for example, coal miners). These short ARA courses trained about 35 thousand persons between October 1961 and December 1964. Three fourths of those trained then found work in the "depressed area" where they were trained and where they could not find work previously.

The Manpower Development and Training Act (MDTA) was passed in 1962 to educate workers in all parts of the country and to educate them more thoroughly than do the programs under ARA. MDTA courses last up to 2 years for people who need to

---

[5] Alan B. Batchelder, "Economic Forces Serving the Ends of the Negro Protest," *The Annals*, January 1965, pp. 86–87.

learn the three R's as well as an occupation. Trainees receive an allowance equal to local unemployment compensation plus, in cases of special need, an extra $10 a week. Workers in OJT programs, set up especially for MDTA, receive smaller allowances because they must be paid by the employer for work on goods and services that the employer sells. Of the 229 thousand MDTA trainees in 1964, almost 28 thousand were in special OJT programs, about 172 thousand were in training other than with employers, and 30 thousand were in "experimental-demonstration projects" for persons with "particularly difficult work problems" (for example, migratory workers, isolated Eskimo and Aleut fishermen, youths in houses of correction, persons 51 years of age or older, and illiterates). MDTA has concentrated upon the long-term unemployed; excluding OJT programs, 40% had been unemployed 15 weeks or more, 29% had been unemployed 6 months or more prior to training. In the first 3 years of the MDTA program, nearly 300 thousand persons were trained.

E. *Increase in Human Capital: "The War on Poverty"*

In 1964, the Johnson Administration called for a crusade against poverty. The core of its War on Poverty was the Economic Opportunity Act of 1964 which provided a new series of programs designed to replace assistance payments with arrangements that permitted the poor to *work* their way out of poverty. A small fraction of the funds used in these programs has been going to help elderly and mentally retarded persons not in the labor force, but most of the money is supposed to be used to reduce poverty by raising the productivity of the poor, thereby increasing the national product.

The statistics and quotations that follow pertain to the various programs of the War on Poverty. The quotations have all been taken from "Examination of the War on Poverty Program" (Hearings before the Subcommittee on the War on Poverty Program, House Committee on Education and Labor, April 12-30, 1965, pp. 81-320). The statistics have all been taken from a statement released by Sargent Shriver, the Director of the Office of Economic Opportunity, on January 22, 1966. Together, they give a clear picture of the Administration's battle strategy.

The *Job Corps* provides residential camps—or schools—that offer "a program of remedial education and job training" for youths 16 to 21 years of age. The program is designed to provide these youths with the "basic minimum requirements of aptitudes, health and ambition that will enable them to" earn their way out of poverty. In general, the program is a second chance for dropouts.

The selection process seeks "those youths who can most benefit from the Job Corps." They work in the camps and are taught reading (not "Jane and Dick" but job manuals), arithmetic (paying taxes, paying other bills), and job skills, *and* they are explicitly taught *to try* to get ahead on the job. Most centers are run by nonprofit agencies; some are run by corporations, for example, Packard-Bell, I.B.M., I.T.T., and Litton Industries. The enrollees average one year of education and work in the camps. Local businessmen's councils help the graduates find work.

The planned enrollment and financing are shown in Table 10-5.

Table 10-5

	July 1965 to June 1966	July 1966 to June 1967
Enrollment	30,000	45,000
Financing	$240,000,000	$355,000,000
Cost per enrollee	$8,000 (includes initial building costs)	$7,890

The *Neighborhood Youth Corps* "provides full- or part-time work experience and training for youths (aged 16 to 21), enabling them to stay in or return to school, or increase their employability" without returning to school. The main feature of the program is work training. Enrollees work under close supervision that, nevertheless, frees the supervising specialists for other work while providing the students with a cash income and preparing them for independent employment. Enrollees in school full time may work up to 16 hours a week. Enrollees not in school may work up to 33 hours a week, then must give at least 4 hours a week to counseling and remedial education.

The planned enrollment and financing are shown in Table 10-6.

Table 10-6

	July 1965 to June 1966	July 1966 to June 1967
Enrollment	100,000 in-school 60,000 out-of-school 165,000 summer	125,000 in-school 64,000 out-of-school 165,000 summer
Financing	$245,000,000	$275,000,000
Cost per enrollee	$754	$777

Work Experience Programs "provide up to 100% funds for projects to help unemployed parents with dependent children, and other needy persons, gain planned and constructive work experience and training interwoven with basic literacy, adult education, and vocational instruction, and a wide range of social services so that they become self-supporting." Nursing-home attendant, practical nurse, stenographer, hospital orderly, and clerk are examples of occupations for which these people train. In addition, they attend classes to learn the three R's and to learn about good work habits.

The planned enrollment and financing are shown in Table 10-7.

Table 10-7

	July 1965 to June 1966	July 1966 to June 1967
Enrollment	109,000	105,000 with 300,000 dependents
Financing	$130,000,000	$160,000,000
Cost per student	$1,190	$1,430

Adult Basic Education programs are "designed to recruit and bring instruction to the largest feasible number of poor adults with the greatest educational definciencies." A variety of new books has been introduced by government administrators and by private publishers to teach the three R's to adults. The market is large; in 1964, there were in the labor force 2.5 million adults who had not completed the fifth grade.

The planned enrollment and financing are shown in Table 10-8.

Rural Loans "provide loan assistance and management advice to low-income farm and nonfarm rural families who need small amounts of capital to improve their earnings but are unable to

Table 10-8

	July 1965 to June 1966	July 1966 to June 1967
Enrollment	75,000	75,000
Financing	$20,000,000	$30,000,000
Cost per enrollee	$267	$400

obtain credit from other sources." Most of these loans go to people too old and unskilled to retrain and too young for Old Age Assistance. Loans up to $2500 are made at 4½% for as long as 15 years. Farmers buy a mule or fertilizer, or clear land; nonfarmers buy a used pickup truck or replace a sledge and wedges with a mechanical log splitter to increase the productivity of the borrower.

The planned lending and financing are shown in Table 10-9.

Table 10-9

	July 1965 to June 1966	July 1966 to June 1967
Borrowers	15,000 individual loans 350 co-op loans	15,500 individual loans 400 co-op loans
Financing	$35,000,000	$38,000,000
Outlay per borrower (not "cost" since most of the money will be repaid)	$2,210	$2,390

✓ *Community Action Programs* "provide financial support for local anti-poverty campaigns in urban and rural areas, on Indian reservations, and among minority workers. Projects include: remedial reading, literacy instruction, job development, vocational rehabilitation, health services, among others. Federal assistance depends on communities' determination to administer and coordinate the community action programs through public or private nonprofit agencies, or a combination of these and involve the poor themselves in developing and operating anti-poverty attacks." The last phrase in the quotation—the requirement for participation by the poor—caused the most controversy during the first year of the program. Established political leaders in the cities of Los Angeles and Syracuse attracted particular attention by resisting the creation of poverty boards with power to disburse millions of dollars free from control of the elected officials in city halls.

The most publicized Community Action Program was *Head Start*, the preschool program that enrolled 560 thousand preschoolers in the summer of 1965 at a cost of $238 million, or $442 per student for instruction, equipment, and food. Additional Community Action Programs teach literacy, other remedial education, child care, and homemakers' services (how to shop economically, nutrition, budgeting). Still other programs provide health services, legal aid, day-care centers for mothers and migratory laborers, housing and education for migrant laborers, counseling for Indian youth, and birth control clinics.

The planned coverage and financing are shown in Table 10-10.

Table 10-10

	July 1965 to June 1966	July 1966 to June 1967
Communities	700	900
Summer Headstart	500,000	500,000
Academic year Headstart	100,000	100,000
Financing	$491,000,000	$735,000,000

Volunteers in Service to America (Vista) "provides an opportunity for Volunteers, 18 and over, to join the War on Poverty. Volunteers work with migratory laborers, on Indian reservations, in urban and rural community action programs, in slum areas, hospitals, schools, and in institutions for the mentally ill and retarded." Volunteers serve one year each. Some teach the three R's. Others help with relocation preceding urban renewal, speech therapy, vocational training of the mentally-retarded, day-care centers, counseling, and home visits to the blind, elderly, and disabled.

The planned enlistment and financing are shown in Table 10-11.

Table 10-11

	July 1965 to June 1966	July 1966 to June 1967
Enlistment	3,500	4,500
Financing	$14,000,000	$23,000,000
Cost per volunteer	$4,000	$5,100

Most of the programs in the War on Poverty contribute directly to the growth of America's human capital. This is one of the three means by which the productivity figures in Table 10-3 increase from year to year. The other two means are technological change and the accumulation of physical capital. The War on Poverty programs are distinctive because they concentrate so narrowly upon increasing productivity *only* among the poor.

IV. SUMMARY

Whereas Chapter 9 described existing arrangements that reduce the incidence of poverty by transferring part of the nation's output from high-income to low-income households, this chapter has described existing arrangements that reduce the incidence of poverty by increasing output per person. Output per person is increased through more complete utilization of existing productive resources, through moderation of the rate of population growth relative to the rate of growth of total output, and through growth in the total quantity of productive resources.

In the years ahead, existing productive resources will be used more completely as Americans' knowledge of the labor market improves, as workers and industry become more mobile, as racial and ethnic discrimination diminish, and—most important—as monetary and fiscal policy induce aggregate demand to press the economy toward full employment. Birth control, by restricting the growth of population, will increase the size of the per capita NNP associated with any given total NNP. The quantity of productive resources will be increased as innovations improve technology, and as the per capita quantity of physical capital and the per capita quantity of human capital grow. The accumulation of human capital—of education—will depend upon what happens in homes, in elementary and secondary schools, and in adult education. The Johnson Administration's War on Poverty will concentrate upon human capital and will contribute to the education of about 1 million poor people each year.

PART *V*

CHOICES FOR AMERICANS

11

The Issues Remain

At the outset of this book we asserted that the best economy would maximize individual freedom of choice. As the means to achieve this maximization, we recommended private ownership of the tools of production, competition among large numbers of sellers and among large numbers of buyers, and a minimum of government and private monopolistic controls. We recommended these means because they provide entrepreneurs, employers, and employees with an ever-expanding range of choice in maximally paid investment and work opportunities, and they provide buyers with a similarly expanding range of choice of minimally priced goods and services. The American economy does not, in all of its parts, satisfy all of these conditions; but, in general, it *is* a privately competitive market economy, and it *does* provide a growing freedom of choice for most Americans.

Within this context, poverty appears as a condition that limits freedom of choice among the poor. First, the poor are limited because they have little money to spend for goods and services. Second, most of them are limited in choice because they have little formal education and are ignorant of the job market and elementary consumer economics. Finally, many American poor have their freedom of choice abridged by physical infirmity, disease, or racial discrimination.

To recap briefly: In our analysis of the economics of poverty

167

in America, we began with an investigation of the extent of poverty in the mid-1960's. Then we considered at length its many causes, and concluded by describing (in two chapters) the processes and programs at work to reduce the extent of poverty in the United States. The previous discussion has avoided controversy. Now we raise many pertinent issues that will provoke controversy in the future.

One historical trend should be remembered when any of the controversial issues are considered: the process of technological change and capital accumulation has, for centuries, raised productivity and reduced the incidence of poverty. Poverty could not be eliminated in England in 1867, not because employers or the Queen were unkind, but because NNP was physically too small relative to the population. Persistent technological change and capital accumulation have brought us to a time when poverty *could* be eliminated in the United States. This process of technological change and capital accumulation has, decade by decade, reduced the incidence of poverty in the United States. Its continuance—perhaps unevenly; possibly with occasional relapses—will continue to raise productivity and reduce the incidence of poverty in the United States. Although particular decisions may influence the rate of technological change and capital accumulation, the overall generalization lies outside the arena of public debate.

But the incidence of poverty will also be affected by decisions on issues subject to political debate, issues over which honest men may violently disagree. Many programs exist to heal or to hide poverty. These programs use tens of billions of dollars each year. Many new programs are being proposed. The old programs are not necessarily good just because they exist. The new proposals are not necessarily bad just because they have not been tried. The old programs can be abolished, expanded, or cut back. The proposals for new programs can be accepted in whole or in part, can be modified, or can be rejected. In our discussion we consider some of the issues, but we do not choose. Each individual must choose for himself by combining an analysis of the economics of poverty with his personal system of value judgments regarding good and bad.

The issues are grouped here under five general headings:

discrimination, taxes, transfers, government spending on goods and services, and the full employment–price stability dilemma.

I. DISCRIMINATION

In the United States there are some white employers who dislike Negroes and who will refuse to hire them even when this refusal reduces company profits. These employers lose some of their freedom of choice when legislation compels them to hire on the basis of ability rather than on the basis of race.

There are white members of American school boards who, disliking Negroes, will allocate money without reference to the Intelligence B of Negro students and who will arbitrarily provide more dollars per student to white schools than to Negro schools. These whites lose some of their freedom of choice when legislation compels them to allocate money on the basis of student potential rather than on the basis of race.

In America's market economy a man's freedom of choice depends upon his access to education, jobs, and money to spend. Legislation compelling white school boards to allocate funds on the basis of student potential rather than on the basis of race increases Negro learning, thereby widening Negro freedom of choice. Legislation compelling employers (and unions and employment agencies) to open jobs on the basis of ability rather than race also widens Negro freedom of choice. Reduced discrimination in education and in employment for Negroes, Indians, Puerto Ricans, and white persons of Spanish surname would, by expanding educational and employment freedom, provide many minority group members with opportunities to work their way out of poverty. But legislation to reduce educational and employment discrimination can work only by abridging the freedom of the white school board members, the white employers, the white employment agency officers, and the white union leaders who want to discriminate against Negroes and members of other minorities. Is such legislation desirable?

Minority groups pay 10 to 25% more than majority-group whites for urban housing of any given quality. The difference is not a result of conspiratorial landlord greed. Instead, it results from white prejudice that limits the number of urban houses and apartments available to Negroes or other minority groups. Whites may buy or rent any house or apartment in town (if they can afford it). Negroes have access to only a portion of the houses and apartments in each American city. Consequently, they bid up prices and rents in their ghetto areas, and Negro dollars become second-class money, which buys less housing, dollar for dollar, than white dollars buy.

Effective "fair housing" legislation would expand the portion of urban residential housing available to minority groups; it would reduce minority-group housing costs, thereby reducing the second-class value of minority-group dollars. This legislation would expand the freedom of minority groups; it would curb the freedom of the many majority-group whites who very much want to discriminate against minority groups in housing. Is such legislation desirable?

No matter what decisions are reached, or what actions are taken respecting racial discrimination, all white Americans and all Negro Americans must anticipate that because of the large numbers of Negroes with $6.67 a year educations, another 40 to 60 years must elapse before Negro education and training *averages* can rise to match the averages of whites.

II. TAX MIX, DEDUCTIONS, AND TAX RATES

In Chapter 9 we learned that sales-excise and property taxes take a larger portion of the income of the poor than of the nonpoor, while federal income taxes take a larger portion of the income of the nonpoor. If we assume a constant total tax collection, it follows that an increase of a fraction in the collection of sales-excise and property taxes and a drop in the portion from income taxes would increase the share of taxes borne by the poor and reduce the share borne by the nopoor. This happens when the federal income tax is cut while sales and property taxes are increased. On the other hand, if federal income taxes were to provide relatively more of the total tax collection, the share of taxes borne by the poor would fall. Should there be a change?

The poor would also be affected by changes in the exemption system and the tax-rate structure. Exempting elderly families from school property taxes would relieve the elderly poor of their heaviest tax burden. Poor families with taxable income would benefit from an increase in the present exemption of $600 a dependent or from a reduction in the rate of taxation upon the first $1000 of income after deductions. Are the present tax mix, exemption system, and rate structure the "best," or should there be changes? A proposed change that could have been considered in this section is the "negative income tax." Because it involves transfers, it is considered under the next category.

III. TRANSFER PAYMENTS

Referring back to Chapter 9, several pertinent questions were raised. Should private transfers be larger and government transfers smaller? Would the United States be a better place if they were? These two questions generate one other question: How likely is it that private transfers to the poor would increase if government transfers were reduced? No matter how we choose to answer this question, present trends appear likely to continue, with private transfers becoming increasingly institutionalized. The answer may depend upon the ability of high-income households to identify and feel a personal obligation to low-income households.

With respect to government transfers, the most fundamental question is: Should there be *any* government transfer payments at all? The availability of government transfers does lead some people to work less than they would otherwise; the higher general relief payments are (relative to the consumer price index) and the easier that it is to obtain general relief, the greater will be the number of people who choose relief over work.[1] The importance of this effect is a matter of opinion. Nevertheless, if we favor government transfer payments, issues arise as to who should receive aid, how payments should be made, and how much each qualifying person should receive.

A recent proposal called for a "Guaranteed Annual Income" through a transfer program that would guarantee every Ameri-

---

[1] Carl T. Brehm and T. R. Saving, "The Demand for General Assistance Payments," *The American Economic Review*, December 1964, pp. 1002–1018.

can family a minimum annual income.[2] For example, a non-farm family of 2 adults and 2 children might be guaranteed $3130 a year; a family with 3 children might receive $535 more. An unattached nonfarm woman might be guaranteed $1525 a year. (These examples use the SSA poverty minima.)

The guarantee program might be operated through state and local governments or through the federal Internal Revenue Service (IRS). In the latter case, if a nonfarm family of 4 reported an income of $2930 for a year, the IRS would send it a check for $200; if its reported income had been $300, the check (or checks) would be for $2830. If such a program were inaugurated with guarantees near the levels suggested, the program would be radical, not because it guaranteed a minimum income, but because it would place the guaranteed income at a relatively high level. The many programs of transfer payments described in Chapter 9 actually provide the poor with a "guaranteed" income between $1000 and $2000 a year. The proposal for a guaranteed annual income is, therefore, not a proposal for something unprecedented; it is a proposal for a big *increase* in government transfers to the poor.

There would be mechanical problems. For example, if the IRS were the administering agency, should the government payment be in a lump sum or spread out over 6 monthly checks, 12 monthly checks, or 52 weekly checks? Should income-reporting to the IRS be on an annual basis or on a semiannual or quarterly basis to reduce the need for a short-run public assistance program?

The chief advantage of the guarantee system would be its potential simplicity, since it would pose only three questions (four if assets were also to be examined):

1. Is this return for one person or for a family?
2. If for a family, how many persons living together and pooling their income?
3. What is the total family income?

---

[2] See, for example, Robert Theobald, "Guaranteeing an Income," *Commonweal*, 4 September 1964, pp. 603–606, and National Commission on Technology, Automation, and Economic Progress, *Technology and the American Economy*, U.S. Government Printing Office, Washington, D.C., 1966.

The administrators would then compare the reported income with the appropriate guaranteed minimum and pay the difference. Programs such as Aid to the Blind, Aid to the Aged, Aid to Families of Dependent Children, and general relief could all be abolished (except for a program for short-run loan aid) along with their means tests and staffs. Administrative costs would be less under this guarantee program than in present transfer programs, but the total cost, depending on the minima guaranteed, could be higher to the nonpoor. Should the United States provide all citizens with a higher guaranteed annual income? If so, how high should the guarantee be and by whom should the program be administered?

The proposal for a "negative income tax" is a version of the income guarantee concept. The negative income tax would provide a guaranteed income that would vary from household to household according to the number of dependents and the earned income of the household. The negative income tax is like other income guarantee proposals in that it could be administered simply and could vary the income guarantee as the earned income varied. In this way, the household would receive an increase in net income whenever it received any increase in earned income. By this provision, the negative income tax would combine income minima with an inducement to recipients to earn their way out of poverty.

Table 11-1 How a Negative Income Tax Plan Might Work for a Man with a Wife and Two Children

With an Earned Income of:	He Would Be This Far Below the Poverty Line:	His Negative Tax Rate Would Be:	His Subsidy Would Equal:	And His After-Income Tax Income Would Be:
None	$3000	50%	$1500	$1500
$500	2500	45	1125	1625
1000	2000	38	750	1750
1500	1500	33	500	2000
2000	1000	25	250	2250
2500	500	25	125	2625
2800	200	25	50	2850
3000	0	0	0	3000

Source. Data from Robert J. Lampman as presented in *Business Week,* November 13, 1965, p. 105.

The mechanics of the proposal are illustrated by Table 11-1, which shows how the plan could work for a man and woman with 2 children with earned income below the poverty line of $3000. When the family's earned income rises from none to $1000, its after-income-tax income would rise $250; the next $1000 increase in earned income would raise its after-income-tax income $500; and the next $1000 increase in earned income would raise its after-income-tax income $750. A different table would be required to show the effects upon households containing more or fewer people. Should such a program be adopted? If so, what should the negative tax rates be?

Other changes are possible. The present public assistance programs (Aid to the Aged, Aid to the Blind, Aid to Dependent Children) and general assistance and the insurance programs for unemployment, work injuries, and old age and survivors could be expanded or cut back. All could be changed; or some could be changed while others were held constant. Should the aged receive less? Should the blind receive more? Should children receive more or less?

IV. GOVERNMENT SPENDING ON GOODS AND SERVICES

Chapter 10 described the activities of the State Employment Service offices. These offices help to bring workers and job openings together, but should the offices do more or less than they do at present?

The Committee on Economic Development, composed of 15 prominent educators and 185 senior officers of the nation's largest corporations, promotes research and discussion to strengthen "our free society" and stimulate rising productivity and "greater opportunity for all our people." In September 1965, the Research and Policy Committee of the CED issued a statement that included several paragraphs evaluating employment service operations. The Committee made the following observation.

. . . the public employment service should provide information on probable future demands for labor, as a guide to the development of training programs. The service should be available to supply more specific counseling to young people and retrained adults about to begin the search for employment.

In general, the public employment service should be a means for prompt nation-wide transmission of accurate information about available workers and available jobs. As a group, our state employment services are not performing this function adequately now. They are still too much concentrated on local needs. In 1963 shifts of workers between areas accounted for only two percent of all non-agricultural placements by the state employment services. They do not adequately test the abilities of job seekers or analyze jobs registered with them. They do not use the capacities of modern computers for storing, classifying, and communicating information. Insufficient effort is devoted to training professional personnel of the employment service.[3]

Two groups—the Special Task Force appointed by the Secretary of Labor, and the President's National Commission on Technology, Automation and Economic Progress—have called for the complete federalization of the employment service and for a federal computer system to match men and jobs. But *should* the employment service be given the money required to obtain more accurate information regarding future demands for labor and to provide more counseling for young people and retrained adults? Should each employment service office provide workers with more extensive information regarding job openings out of its immediate area? Should the employment service be given the money required to test more applicants and to classify jobs in terms of essential employee qualifications? Should the employment service be given additional money to invest in training more professional workers for jobs in the service? In short, should more money go to the employment service to make it more efficient in bringing workers and job openings together so that the nonpoor may more easily avoid and the poor more easily escape poverty? Or are the prospective gains insufficient to justify the higher costs?

A. *Geographic Mobility*

Chapter 10 considered some existing government programs that help finance the geographic movement of workers and businesses. The Federal Government is experimentally using grants and loans to help workers move from areas of job scarcity

---

[3] Committee for Economic Development, *Raising Low Incomes through Improved Education,* New York, September 1965, p. 37.

to areas of labor shortage in private employment. Should this program be continued? Should it be expanded? Should both loans and grants be provided, or should the program be limited to loans?

The Area Redevelopment Administration has helped communities obtain new factories. In 1964, the voters of Ohio approved their governor's proposal to create a "socialized" state bank to make cheap industrial loans in order to attract industry from Southern states, which make similar offers through state-owned banks. Should governments, federal, state, or local, provide money to help selected (poor?) communities expand old plants or obtain new plants? In nearly every case, the new production facility, obtained with government help, would have been built elsewhere in the absence of government intervention. If the new plant had been built elsewhere, the unemployed of the poor community *could* have moved to the other location—although they might have been reluctant to do so. Should the governor of a state or the director of a federal agency be allowed to use public money to divert production facilities to places he favors?

Some of the poor of depressed rural areas do not want to move. A private front porch, a wide expanse of trees, wild game, clean running water, and space cannot be obtained in the city. These attractions are highly valued by people who derive much of their satisfaction from watching their children and then their grandchildren mature. Even though the dollars remaining from an urban paycheck after paying for urban rent and food may be well above available rural earnings, many of these people prefer to stay put—although, as pointed out in Chapter 10, many *are* moving. Should jobs be brought to those who choose to remain? Should they receive other special attention?

B. *Adult Education*

Adult education was once an exclusively private affair. It no longer is. Many school districts offer adult-education courses. Some districts charge fees high enough to cover all operating expenses; some levy only nominal charges and pay other expenses from school tax receipts. States now provide funds for adult-training programs. In the Manpower Development and

Training Act, the Federal Government undertook to finance adult education. How much adult education and training *should* government taxes provide? Which levels of government, if any, should participate?

Every school district offers twelve years of free schooling. How much more *should* government provide? Every state subsidizes four additional years of school for those who care to go to college. Furthermore, parents who send their children beyond college to professional school (for example, to a law school) can do so at public expense by sending their children to a state university. There is no "need" test; any family choosing this route is able to benefit by having the powerful state tax all citizens—poor as well as nonpoor—to obtain the funds used to subsidize their sons' or daughters' advanced specialized education.

Should the state do this? There is no issue; all states do, and there is no criticism. Having taxed the poor to help pay the educational costs of advanced degrees for the nonpoor, *should* the state, school district, city or Federal Government tax the nonpoor to provide testing, counseling, education, and training for adults who are poor but who are neither qualified for nor interested in a state-run professional school? An alternative having the same implications for equity would be to reduce state taxes and end state tax support for professional schools. Could public support be rallied for such a move?

The War on Poverty programs represent a new burst of effort to educate poor adults and, to a lesser extent, to educate the children of the poor. During 1965, Congressmen referred to the program as an experiment testing various means to help the poor work their way out of poverty. Is the experiment worthwhile? Should it be continued? How are we to judge?

The War-on-Poverty budget of a $1.5 billion a year is administered by tens of thousands of people. Inevitably among fallible men, some portion of this budget (of which 1% is $15 million) will be spent in extravagant conflict with the legislative intent of the program. In the months since the program received initial funding in October 1964, newspapers have headlined some spectacular misallocations of funds. These wastes require consideration when one weighs the overall product-to-cost effects, but the net worth of the program can be determined only with full information regarding the costs and the short- and long-run effects of the entire program. In early 1965, the Office of Economic Opportunity, which administers the "War," created a "weapons evaluation division" to measure the poverty-reducing results of $1 million spent on Vista, $1 million spent on the Job Corps, $1 million spent on the Neighborhood Youth Corps, and so on for the other projects. As the findings of this analysis become available, the public may obtain access to data measuring the "productivity" of dollars spent on each project. This information will help voters decide which programs to expand, which to hold constant, which to cut back, and which to abolish.

C. *Public Elementary and Secondary Schools*

As a rule of thumb in the United States, schools attended by the children of poor families are inferior in teachers, equipment, and course variety when compared with schools attended by the children of nonpoor families. Public policy may react to this difference in one of three ways.

Choice 1. The difference can be maintained, with the nonpoor continuing in schools superior to the schools of the poor.

Choice 2. School boards can allocate funds among schools in direct proportion to the average number of pupils in daily attendance.

Choice 3. Extra money can be provided for schools of children of the poor so that these schools can approximately compensate for defects of home and neighborhoods. The prospect would then be that the nonpoor child and the poor child of equal Intelligence B would attain equal Intelligence C.

If Choice 2 were adopted, then equal funds per student would represent equal state educational effort per child during school hours, but home and neighborhood environments would contribute much less to the education of the poor than to the education of the nonpoor. Equal tax dollars per attending pupil in poor and in nonpoor schools would, therefore, not yield equal results. Given equal Intelligence B, the children of the poor would learn less in total than the children of the nonpoor, especially

in those subjects having value in the market and in ideas con-
stituting good citizenship. Thus, the Intelligence C of the
nonpoor child would rise farther above his Intelligence B than
would the Intelligence C of the poor child. In contrast, Choice
3 would elicit a different result.

Which of these choices *should* be adopted by the school
boards of the United States? Should the 1965 Congressional
commitment to help children from poor families "catch up" be
repealed, or should it be ratified by adopting Choice 3? If either
Choice 2 or 3 were to be adopted, should it apply only within
each school district? Or should funds be allocated to permit
equalization among all schools in a metropolitan area? Or
in a state? Or in the nation?

Even if most school boards continue to adhere to Choice 1,
vocational education will continue to provoke controversy. The
Committee for Economic Development recently concluded that
"the vocational education programs of our schools, mainly
high schools, have been seriously deficient," teaching "outdated or declining occupations, by outdated methods on outdated equipment."[4] Should more money be spent to match
courses, methods, and equipment with the prospective market?
Should more money be spent to provide more vocational counseling? More vocational classes? More vocational school buildings?

In schools for children of poor families, caution should be
exercised when anticipating the children's potential. The qualities valued in the United States market are, in part hereditary.
It may be that most of the poor have had their chance and became poor because of limited Intelligence A. If so, their children would inherit genes of limited potential.

In this respect, there may be a great difference between Negroes and whites—and, more generally, between minority groups
and the white majority. It may be that most poor whites are
poor because low Intelligence A led them to fail when given a
chance in school and in the employment market. Negroes are
in a much different position. Relatively few have been given

---

[4] Committee for Economic Development, *Raising Low Incomes through
Improved Education,* New York, September 1965, pp. 25–26.

an equal chance either in school or in the job market. Thus, poverty comes to some Negroes because of low Intelligence A, whereas it comes to other Negroes because of discrimination and in spite of high Intelligence A and high Intelligence B. If these generalizations are true, children of the white poor will, on the average, have lower Intelligence A than children of the Negro poor. And, if the differences in Intelligence B are not too unlike the differences in Intelligence A, money spent educating the children of the Negro poor will yield higher productive returns than if spent educating the children of the white poor. If these conclusions are correct, *should* more money per neighborhood child be put into schools of the Negro poor than into schools of the white poor?

Some commentators have argued that schools for children from poor families, especially for children from poor minority-group families, are inferior because (1) the teachers do not expect the children to learn, (2) the school administrators do not expect the teachers to teach, and (3) the teachers suffer no penalty if their children do not learn. To counteract these conditions, the salary in teachers' renewal contracts could be determined by the *percentage* of increase in average scores on standardized tests taken by their students at the beginning, the middle, and the end of the school year. The percentage rule would mean that students rising 5 points from a score of 50 to a score of 55 would justify a salary increase equal to that justified by a rise of 10 points between scores of 100 and 110 points. Thus, the system would work with slow classes as well as with brighter classes. Should teachers be paid in proportion to their accomplishments? Should the system suggested here be used to elicit better teaching in schools attended by children of poor families?

D. *Birth Control*

In 1963, the SSA criteria counted 7.2 million poor families with 14.7 million adults and 15 million children under 18. One half of the 15 million children lived in homes with 5 or more *other* children. Exactly 40% of the poor children lived in families in which at least 1 family member worked full time all year during 1963. These families combined low adult productivity—in employment—with high birth rates. Adults held jobs but, with low productivity, these people produced and earned little. Given low productivity—or unemployment— families already poor could avoid severe poverty by practicing birth control. The potentially poor might escape poverty altogether by restricting the growth of their families.

The arithmetic and economics of birth control as a means of reducing poverty are straightforward. The moral issues remain. Should governments provide birth control information and devices to the poor who request them? Should governments provide this information and these devices to unmarried women? Should governments advertise to encourage the poor to practice birth control? The answers to these questions will affect a majority of the poor in the United States. If the answer in each instance is "no," what alternative policies are appropriate?

E. *Public Transportation*

The recent riots in the Watts area of Los Angeles called nationwide attention to an urban area of many square miles lacking any means of public transportation. The Watts situation appeared to typify a developing big-city pattern in which public transportation is arranged to connect the middle-class suburbs with the central city mercantile and industrial centers, while leaving the innercity low-income areas without means of transportation, except private autos or feet.

It is not enough for a man to be able to do a job, nor is it enough for him to know of a job that he can do—he must be able to *get to* the job. Should city councils insist that public transportation agencies service the ghettos and other low-income areas? If so, should transit fees cover the operating costs, or should the transportation lines be subsidized? If they should be subsidized, which level of government should provide the money?

F. *Mothers with Dependent Children*

Government-financed day-care centers are being set up in many urban areas to permit a woman to leave her children in institutional care while she takes a job as a supplementary income earner or as the sole source of earned income for her family.

Are day-care centers a good arrangement? Is it better (1) to leave these mothers with poverty-level transfers, (2) to have the mothers home with their children and receiving from the nonpoor transfers large enough to lift themselves out of poverty, or (3) to separate the mothers from the children 8 to 9 hours a day while the mothers work and the children remain in institutional care?

G. Federal, or State, or Local?

Quite apart from the questions raised earlier regarding tax rates and the "proper" mix of sales-excise, income, and property taxes, two questions arise whenever government intervention is proposed. Should government revenue come from federal, from state, or from local taxes? Should the program be administered by the Federal Government, or by state or by local governments? Beyond questions of "should" is the query: *Would* one level of government be willing to assume taxing and administrative responsibility for a program being phased out by another level of government? For example, would the states be willing to accept taxing and administrative responsibility for a particular program if the Federal Government were to withdraw from intervention in that area?

V. FULL EMPLOYMENT OR PRICE STABILITY

Chapter 4 pointed to the positive correlation between unemployment rates and the incidence of poverty. In the short run, the relationship simply involves the availability of opportunities to earn income. But unemployment levels also influence business decisions regarding both the investment in physical capital and the expenditures on research leading to technological improvements, which increase the size of NNP in the long run. When unemployment is high, research and net investment expenditures are low. Net private domestic investment was $46.2 billion in 1965; it was −$6.4 billion in 1932 when depreciation exceeded gross investment. Unemployment levels also affect the accumulation of education, which increases the size of NNP in the long run. During the 1930's, many Americans failed to obtain the on-the-job training, the apprenticeship training, the general work experience, the college or even the high school education they would have obtained if unemployment rates had been lower. The higher the unemployment rate is, the smaller the NNP, and the higher is the incidence of poverty—in the short run. Furthermore, the less the amount of research that is done, the less will be the accumulation of physical and human capital—in the long run—and the smaller will be the NNP, and the higher will be the incidence of poverty.

A. *The Dilemma*

The difficulty is that the United States can have full employment (reduced incidence of poverty) and inflation *or* stable prices and relatively high unemployment (higher incidence of poverty). There is no conflict between price stability and unemployment rates of 8 or even 7½%—but below 6%, conflict arises. The United States cannot have full employment *and* stable prices. Most Americans view with equal displeasure each horn of this dilemma of high inflation or high unemployment (and greater poverty). But the dilemma is unavoidable given the conditions of the American market of the 1960's.

The term "full employment" immediately suggests that 100% of the people in the labor force are employed while 0% are unemployed. But in the United States (as was pointed out in Chapter 10), the high mobility of workers between jobs keeps so many people in motion that most economic commentators accept 3% unemployment as representing full employment. "Price stability" is a less troublesome concept. It does not mean that all prices remain constant. It means that price cuts on some items are exactly offset by increases on other items so that average prices remain perfectly stable.

A full-employment rate of 3% unemployment could be reached by the United States, if monetary and fiscal policy were sufficiently expansionary. Indeed, unemployment could be cut to 2% (it dropped to 1.2% in 1944) under a sufficiently expansionary monetary and fiscal policy. An unemployment level of 3% would so enlarge the national product that the number of unemployed would fall considerably, thereby pulling many persons into jobs and out of poverty. The formula is simple: apply monetary-fiscal policies, raise aggregate demand, expand employment, cut unemployment to 3%, and reduce poverty. However, there are "buts." As aggregate demand rises enough in the United States to cut unemployment to low levels, the desires of buyers become so urgent that prices are bid up; this is inflation.

B. *Many Benefit from Inflation, but . . .*

Inflation means that buyers pay higher prices to sellers who distribute their higher incomes in wages, salaries, rent, interest, and profits. Whatever is paid in higher prices is received by someone as higher income. If an inflation is so great that prices double and the national product of one year costs twice as much as the national product of *equal quantity* in an earlier year, then incomes will also be doubled. If prices double and incomes double, who cares? Who would be hurt?

In this example, prices double—on the average—and incomes double—on the average. But not all prices double; some rise more, some less. Neithr do all incomes double; some rise more, some rise less. If all prices rose equally, if all incomes rose equally, *and* if there were no creditors, then inflation would injure no one. But there are creditors and there are fixed-income families, and they are hurt by inflation.

Creditors (a term embracing all savers-lenders) who store $100 in banks, in cash, in life insurance, or in bonds or other loans before prices double do so expecting possession of a future $100 (plus perhaps $5 a year interest). When, following a doubling of prices, the creditor spends his money, the $100 (and the $5 a year interest) buys only one half as much as when the $100 was saved. Thus, the creditors lose. But their loss is exactly equal to the gain of the borrowers. When the borrowers agreed to repayment, they anticipated a sacrifice of purchasing power fully double that required after the inflation. Although the borrowers did nothing to "deserve" the gain, the borrowers do benefit from inflation, and their gain is exactly equal to the loss of the lenders—who did nothing to "deserve" the loss.

A deflation—a drop in prices—has an exactly opposite effect. Deflation robs the borrowers, the booty going to the saver-lenders. But deflation is not an imminent prospect for the

United States,. and consequently is not further considered here.

Inflation robs creditors to benefit debtors. Inflation also robs fixed-income groups to benefit variable-income groups. The sum of price increases during inflation equals the sum of higher incomes. But some people's incomes rise more than the increase in average prices. These people are able to buy more goods and services in an amount equal, to the loss of those whose income rose less than prices. The latter make up the "fixed-income group," a term as awkward as "hard-top convertible." The *convertible* does not *convert*. The income of the *fixed*-income group may *change* (and does change for most people), but a family is part of the fixed-income group if its *percentage* of change in income is less than the *percentage* of change in prices. The variable-income group, embracing those whose percentage of change in income exceeds the percentage of change in prices, does nothing to "deserve" a gain in purchasing power. Yet, this group receives, in benefits, whatever the fixed-income group loses through inflation. A deflation would rob the variable-income group in order to aid the fixed-income group.

High employment brings small pay checks, low profits, a high incidence of poverty, and stable prices. When unemployment rates decline, so does the incidence of poverty; if unemployment falls low enough, then prices rise, and debtors and the variable-income group gain. But creditors and members of the fixed-income group suffer from the inflation, although they may gain from the expansion.

C. *The Unemployment-Price-Change Relationship*

The dilemma of high unemployment *or* rising prices exists because of the relationship shown in Figure 11-1 where yearly unemployment rates of the civilian labor force are compared with the year-to-year percentage of change in the consumer price index (CPI). More precisely, Figure 11-1 plots the unemployment rate for a recession trough year—for example, 5.9% for 1949—against the percentage of change in the CPI between that year and the following year (in this instance, +0.96% between 1949 and 1950). The mean unemployment rate for each set of years between troughs—for example, 4.3%

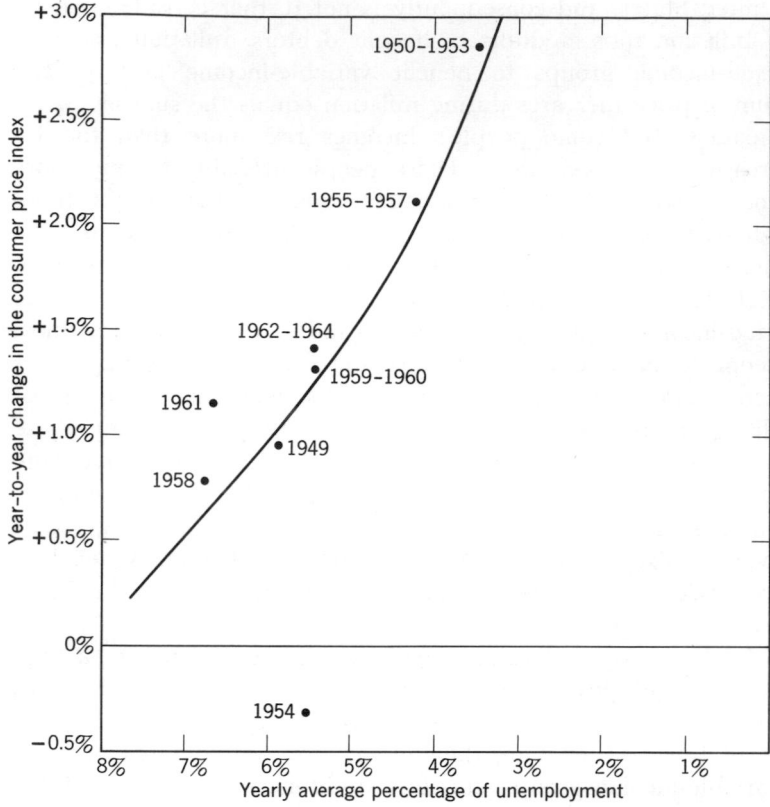

Figure 11-1. The unemployment-level, price-change relationship: 1949 to 1965. (*Source.* Calculated from the *Economic Report of the President: 1966*, U.S. Government Printing Office, Washington, D.C., 1966, pp. 232 and 261.

for the years 1950 to 1953—is plotted against the mean percentage of year-to-year change in the CPI between the pairs of years beginning with the first year after a trough and running through the next trough year (in this example, +2.10% for the pairs of years, 1950 to 1951, 1951 to 1952, 1952 to 1953, and 1953 to 1954). The line sloping upward to the right through the graph shows the approximate year-to-year price changes associated with particular unemployment levels in America. For example, an unemployment rate of about 7½ to 8% would be associated with stable prices. An unemployment rate of 8½% would bring slightly falling prices. An unemployment rate of 5½% would be associated with increases in prices of about 1¼% a year. An unemployment rate of 4½% would bring price increases of about 1¾% a year.

The unemployment measure used here is reliable as a measure of year-to-year *changes* when we understand the definitions used (for example, "full employment"). The CPI used here is currently under attack for failure to allow adequately for improvements in quality. For example, if the life of automobile tires were increased from 15 to 30 thousand miles, a change in single-tire price from $20 to $40 would not represent an increase in tire-mileage price. Changes such as this do occur, and the Bureau of Labor Statistics makes allowances for these changes in quality (up or down), but critics assert that the allowances do not allow fully for quality improvements.

Medical services are an area in which allowance for price changes may be insufficient. Recently, with unemployment at 5½%, the CPI for medical services rose 3½% a year—nearly *three times* the increase for all other goods and services. The statisticians, calculating price changes, allowed for quality improvement in medical services. If they allowed enough, then medical service prices *are* inflating 3½% a year. If they did not, then the price index is rising with increases in unit prices *and* with improvements in the quality of the units. Weighing this issue, one astute commentator has observed as follows.

From a welfare standpoint, one also remembers the probable upward bias of measured price indexes. Very possibly the average price rise of 1.5 per cent in 1958–1963 was matched by or even exceeded by improvements in product quality, so that the value of money did not decline. This assumption would greatly improve the outlook for reconciling full employment with stability in the value of money.

Some economists argue in favor of a more vigorously expansionary policy even if the price level does rise more. They feel the harm done to the unemployed by unemployment is at least as great as the harm done by inflation to those who actually lose by it. And they note that a more expansionary policy means more total output, benefiting many more people than those who might be unemployed.

There seems little doubt, however, that American public opinion tends to react strongly against price increases when they pass (roughly) the 3 per cent level. This was apparent in the political campaign of 1952, for example. Such an attitude may reflect an incomplete balancing of burdens and benefits, but it cannot be ignored.[5]

Perhaps the price index figures in Figure 11-1 overstate price increases by failure to allow enough for quality changes. If so, creditors and the fixed-income group are not injured as much by low unemployment rates as the graph indicates. Nevertheless, subsequent paragraphs accept the price index figures at face value.

D. *Institutional Causes of Rising Prices*

Why do prices rise in the United States long before full employment is reached? One cause is the monopoly power possessed and used by some unions and some businesses. A second cause is employer reluctance to hire able members of minority groups except when labor costs are rising. A third cause is labor immobility that leads to a bidding up first of wages and then of product prices when businesses seek to attract particular kinds of employees away from other employers or other areas. A fourth cause is the custom that some manufacturing industries do not cut prices as rising productivity increases their per capita income, whereas service industries, lacking increases in productivity, frequently raise prices in an effort to achieve the increases in per capita income already going to manufacturing labor, management, and stockholders as a result of rising productivity. Thus, stable prices in manufacturing lead to rising prices in services (health services, for example), and the average price level rises.[6]

E. *The Ideal and the Likely*

The unemployment level—price change relationships, shown in Figure 11-1, derive from a particular period. They are not unchangeable. The line could move farther to the left or farther

---

[5] Paul B. Trescott, *Money, Banking, and Economic Welfare*, 2nd ed., McGraw-Hill, New York, 1965, pp. 171–172.

[6] For a more detailed analysis of the relationships between aggregate demand and prices, see Arnold Collery, *National Income and Employment Analysis*, in this series.

to the right. If the line were to move to the right until it passed through point X, one ideal would become attainable: a condition where high aggregate demand would yield full employment *and* price stability. Improvements in the education of the least-educated portion of the labor force, improvements in labor-force knowledge of work opportunities, improvements in geographic mobility, and reduced racial discrimination would move the line farther to the right.

In an attempt to move the line to the right, the Council of Economic Advisers (in 1962) urged labor and management to observe a set of "wage-price guideposts." The general guidepost for wages is that the annual rate of increase of total employee compensation (wages *and* fringe benefits) per man-hour worked should equal the 3.2% national trend in the rate of increase in man-hour output. The guidepost for prices carries a different instruction for each of the following three kinds of firms.

1. In firms where output per man-hour rises 3.2% a year, prices should be held *constant* while profits, salaries, and wages rise 3.2%.

2. In firms where output per man-hour rises more than 3.2%—for example, chemicals—wages, salaries, and profits should rise only 3.2%,[7] while the rest of the increase in productivity is passed along to buyers in *lower* prices.

3. In firms where output per man-hour rises less than 3.2% a year—for example, medical services—prices are to *rise* just enough to permit profits, salaries, and wages to rise 3.2%.

The guideposts admit a host of exceptions regarding growth industries and declining industries, but would result, in general, in an across-the-board increase of 3.2% a year in wages and salaries, while consumer prices remained perfectly *level* even at low levels of unemployment.

No one expects the guideposts to yield that neat an outcome, but they may be edging the line of Figure 11-1 to the

---

[7] These wage and salary increases are across the board and are separate from increases associated with movement up the escalator of responsibility as older men retire and are replaced by promotion from below.

right. The 1965 to 1966 confrontations between Federal Government stockpiles and defense contracts, and the steel, aluminum, and copper industries have admitted another force that may restrain price increases, thereby shifting the Figure 11-1 line to the right and permitting lower unemployment levels for any given rate of price increases.

For the present, the line rests about where it is shown in Figure 11-1. Recognizing this, how far down *should* aggregate demand press unemployment rates? What rates of price increase shall we tolerate? Answers to these questions will differ between debtors and creditors and between members of the variable-income and the fixed-income groups. They will also depend upon the importance that each person attaches to growth in *total* output.

VI. CONCLUSION

The incidence of poverty in any nation depends upon the total output of the nation and the manner in which that output is distributed. During past decades, so much of annual output went into net investment that, in the 1960's, per capita output in the United States far exceeds the poverty income minima. Out of total NNP, part is diverted to government uses and part to net investment to increase the per capita NNP of the future. Even after diversions to governments and to net investment, the per capita output of the United States remains well above the poverty minima of the 1960's.

In the United States, private output is distributed roughly in proportion to each household's contribution to production. Year by year, the growth in quality and quantity of human and physical capital has increased American NNP by enlarging the productive contribution of most households. This process has been the chief instrumentality by which the incidence of poverty has been reduced in the past, and it will continue to operate in the same way in the future.

The degree of poverty can be cut by increasing transfers from nonpoor to poor households, by reducing the taxes levied on poor households (the taxes can be thought of as negative transfers), or by increasing the productive ability and the productive contribution of poor households. Controversy arises when programs are suggested that would change the size of transfers to the poor, the tax rates of the poor, or the social practices, government spending, or employment levels that affect the productive ability and productive contribution of the poor. Controversy arises because more goods and services for one household so often means fewer goods and services for another.

These conflicts require that American housewives, government officials, investors, employers, and employees must choose. For example, we cannot have freedom for Negroes to work on the basis of ability *and,* at the same time, have freedom for employers to discriminate on the basis of race. We cannot have superior (or even equal) schools in nonpoor areas *and,* at the same time, have kids in schools in poor neighborhoods catching up. We cannot have higher transfers to poor households without leaving nonpoor households with less. We must choose.

Over the long run, the growth of per capita output (the central characteristic of the twentieth century) changes the conflict from "losers versus gainers" to a conflict over how much of the total gain should go to each group. But men live also in the short run. Most nonproductive persons are kept from poverty by intrafamily transfers; yet, there remain more than 30 million Americans who, by the criteria of the SSA, now live in poverty. There are many areas in which public and private actions will move that figure up or down.

In this chapter we have surveyed areas in which there are sharp conflicts. We have not suggested solutions. We have not even offered optional sets of solutions to various combinations of programs, because the possible combinations are too numerous. Americans will experiment with various groupings; some of the proposed programs will not be tried; some will be tried and then abandoned; and others will be tried and modified. Each decision will be reached in the context of its own time.

Weighing the issues under the headings of taxes, transfers, discrimination, government expenditures, and full-employment versus stable prices, how are we to decide what should be done? Honest, intelligent, informed men may disagree. Each person decides on the basis of his own set of values. Economists, considering any proposal, are inclined to take the long view, and then sort the probable short- and long-run effects into those likely to increase the freedom of individuals and those likely to reduce it. By totaling the net value of these effects, a decision can be made on the side maximizing freedom of choice. That is the economists's way, and it represents his bias. Other people may choose differently from a different bias.

What will happen to the incidence of poverty in the United States in the years ahead? In past years, technological change and capital accumulation have trimmed its size. These processes, aided and abetted by rising aggregate demand, will continue to reduce the amount of poverty in the future. Over the short run, institutions and programs will change in ways that will affect both the size of the transfers that can reduce poverty and the ability of the poor to earn their way out of impoverishment. These changes will depend on the decisions of Americans working within the limitations of the existing technology and the existing stock of productive resources. Meanwhile, the immediate issues all come under the general heading: Should the nonpoor majority, through governments or as individuals, do more or do less to alleviate the conditions of the approximately 30 million Americans living in poverty today?

Addresses of Organizations from which Additional Information Can Be Obtained

Federal Government

Equal Employment Opportunity
  Commission
Washington, D. C. 20506

Office of Economic Opportunity
Executive Office of the President
Washington, D. C. 20503

U. S. Bureau of Labor Statistics
Washington, D. C. 20210

U. S. Civil Rights Commission
Washington, D. C. 20425

U. S. Government Printing Office
Washington, D. C. 20402

U. S. Social Security Administration
Washington, D. C. 20201

Private

Center for the Study of Democratic
  Institutions
Box 4068
Santa Barbara, Cal. 93103

Citizens' Crusade Against Poverty
132 Third Street S.E.
Washington, D. C. 20003

Committee for Economic
  Development
1000 Connecticut Avenue N.W.
Washington, D. C. 20036

Committee on Pockets of Poverty
1020 Connecticut Avenue N.W.
Washington, D. C. 20036

Conference on Economic Progress
1001 Connecticut Avenue N.W.
Washington, D. C. 20036

Grey Areas Project
Ford Foundation
477 Madison Avenue
New York, N. Y. 10022

National Association for the
  Advancement of Colored People
20 West 40th Street
New York, N. Y. 10018

National Planning Association
1606 New Hampshire Avenue N.W.
Washington, D. C. 20009

National Sharecroppers Fund
112 East 19th Street
New York, N. Y. 10003

Planned Parenthood
515 Madison Avenue
New York, N. Y. 10022

Research Department
A.F.L.-C.I.O.
815 16th Street, N.W.
Washington, D. C. 20006

Southern Regional Council
5 Forsythe, N.W.
Atlanta, Ga. 30303

Task Force on Economic Growth
  and Opportunity
1615 H Street, N.W.
Washington, D. C. 20006

The W. E. Upjohn Institute for
  Employment Research
709 South Westnedge Avenue
Kalamazoo, Mich. 49007

Annotated Bibliography

The intense activity in the study of poverty over the past few years has led to an abundance of literature on the subject. The selections mentioned in this bibliography represent some of the best work produced in this area. It is hoped that this compilation will inspire both students and teachers to engage in further study of the field. The designation "paper" denotes books available in paperback.

I. GENERAL DISCUSSION AND COLLECTIONS OF READINGS

Bagdikian, Ben H., *In the Midst of Plenty: The Poor in America*, Beacon Press, Boston, 1964, and New American Library (Signet, paper), 1964. This short book contains a dozen dramatic vignettes, each illustrating a different "cause" of poverty. These case studies put flesh on the statistics of poverty.

Dunne, George H. (ed.), *Poverty in Plenty*, P. J. Kenedy and Sons, Washington, D. C., 1964. This is a collection of eight papers (four by economists) presented at the 175th Anniversary Conference, "Poverty-in-Plenty: The Poor in Our Affluent Society," held at Georgetown University in January 1964.

Ferman, Louis A., Joyce L. Kornbluh, and Alan Haber (eds.), *Poverty in America*, University of Michigan Press (paper), 1965. This is the longest collection of readings. Most of the 44 entries are modestly long. The conditions, character, values, and life of the poor are emphasized.

Friedman, Milton, *Capitalism and Freedom*, University of Chicago Press (Phoenix, paper), Chicago, 1962. This book is an eloquent argument for the free man and for the free market as a means to free men. Chapters on the social responsibility of business and labor, the distribution of income, social welfare measures, education, and the alleviation of poverty (this one urging a negative income tax) all argue for a minimum of government intervention.

Harrington, Michael, *The Other America: Poverty in the United States*, The Macmillan Company, New York, 1962, and Penguin Books (paper),

Baltimore, 1963. This book was widely read following its publication. The author, a member of the Catholic Worker movement, set out to inform the nonpoor majority that millions of Americans were poor through no fault of their own.

Kolko, Gabriel, *Wealth and Power in America: An Analysis of Social Class and Income Distribution*, Frederick A. Praeger (paper), New York, 1962. Kolko argues that income inequality is *not* declining in America but *should* be declining. Included is a 12-page bibliography.

MacIver, R. M. (ed.), *The Assault on Poverty: Individual Responsibility*, Harper and Row, New York, 1965. A series of 13 addresses delivered at The Institute for Religious and Social Studies of The Jewish Theological Seminary of America in 1963 to 1964 which consider the causes of poverty and various means to alleviate poverty.

Seligman, Ben B. (ed.), *Poverty as a Public Issue*, The Free Press, New York, 1965. The editor has assembled 13 papers by experts writing about the statistics and characteristics of the poor, about the War on Poverty, and about general criteria for public expenditures on the poor.

Shostak, Arthur V. and William Gomberg (eds.), *New Perspectives on Poverty*, Prentice-Hall (Spectrum, paper), Englewood Cliffs, N. J., 1965. Most of these 19 readings deal with existing or proposed means of alleviating the severity of the incidence of poverty.

Stern, Philip M. and George de Vincent, *The Shame of a Nation*, Obolensky, New York, 1965. An account of American poverty designed to appeal to the emotions.

Weisbrod, Burton A., *The Economics of Poverty: An American Paradox*, Prentice-Hall (Spectrum, paper), Englewood Cliffs, N. J., 1965. Weisbrod has included only 16 readings—mostly by economists—but has tied them together neatly with a tightly argued introductory essay that gives added meaning to each of the parts.

Will, Robert E. and Harold G. Vatter (eds.), *Poverty in Affluence: The Social, Political, and Economic Dimensions of Poverty in the United States*, Harcourt, Brace & World (paper), New York, 1965. The largest collection of readings—72, most of them brief—this book includes 10 articles on the historical ideologies of poverty.

II. STATISTICAL CONSIDERATIONS

Caplovitz, David, *The Poor Pay More: Consumer Practices of Low-Income Families*, The Free Press of Glencoe, New York, 1963. Attention centers upon major durable goods purchases by low-income families in New York. Illegal sales practices receive extended attention as free market devices permitting the least credit-worthy families to buy on credit. Reforms are urged.

Lampman, Robert J., *The Low Income Population and Economic Growth*, prepared as Study Paper 12 for the Joint Economic Committee, Congress of the United States, 86th, 1st, Government Printing Office (paper),

Washington, D. C., 1959. One of the first papers calling attention to the contemporary poor. Lampman describes the decline in the incidence of poverty between 1947 and 1957 and forecasts continued but slower reduction in the incidence of poverty, unless a more aggressive government policy develops.

Miller, Herman P., *Rich Man, Poor Man*, Thomas Y. Crowell Company, New York, 1964, and New American Library (Signet, paper), 1965. Miller, an economist with the Census Bureau for 17 years, evaluates and interprets the income data collected by the Census Bureau. Seventy tables summarize his statistics as he correlates income levels with personal characteristics.

Morgan, James N., Martin H. David, Wilbur J. Cohen, and Harvey E. Brazer, *Income and Welfare in The United States*, McGraw-Hill, New York, 1962. The four authors, all on the staff of the Survey Research Center, Institute for Social Research, University of Michigan, have assembled an elaborately detailed statistical picture of the distribution of earned and transfer income in America and of the personal characteristics of persons in different income groups.

Task Force on Economic Growth and Opportunity, *The Concept of Poverty*, Chamber of Commerce of the United States (paper), Washington, D. C., 1965. The Task Force is made up of over 100 leaders of industry, business, and finance representing major corporations. The Task Force solicits papers from experts and publishes them along with its own recommendations. This volume contains papers by John T. Dunlop, Victory R. Fuchs, Herman P. Miller, and Eugene Smolensky. The recommendations are carefully thought out. Forthcoming volumes in the poverty series will consider the unemployed, the uneducated, the minority group, the farm, and the regional poor and the relationship between population growth and poverty.

U. S. Congress, Joint Economic Committee, 88th, 2d, *The Distribution of Personal Income*, Government Printing Office (paper), Washington, D. C., 1965. This is a technical statistical study of the distribution of personal income among American households.

III. HISTORICAL REPORTS

Bremner, Robert H., *From the Depths: The Discovery of Poverty in The United States*, New York University Press (paper), New York, 1956. Bremner concentrates upon the years between mid-nineteenth century and mid-1920's. Most of the book is devoted to the changes, and causes of changes, in the attitude toward the poor among legislators, writers of fiction, and the nonpoor generally. A 37-page bibliography concludes the book.

Riis, Jacob A., *The Battle with the Slum*, The Macmillan Company, New York, 1902. This immigrant journalist, in his earlier book *How the Other Half Lives*, was the first to tell many middle-class Americans about their slums. In the first-cited book he reported on progress made at the beginning of the century against slums and Tammany.

Riis, Jacob A., *How the Other Half Lives: Studies among the Tenements of New York*, reprinted by Sagamore Press, New York, 1957, and Hill and Wang (American Century, paper), New York, 1957. The police reporter for the *Tribune* and *Sun* used this book to carry his message to the people outside the slums—including President Roosevelt. Assimilation was his goal, education his means.

IV. THE SLUMS

Schorr, Alvin L., *Slums and Social Insecurity*, Government Printing Office, (paper), Washington, D. C., 1963. Schorr describes the conditions of slum housing and considers the effects of government housing programs.

Hunter, David R., *The Slums: Challenge and Response*, Free Press of Glencoe, New York, 1964. Hunter provides a comprehensive and reliable description of the condition of American urban slums and of their residents in the 1960's, and he offers an encompassing survey of actions that would moderate the extent and condition of these areas.

V. POVERTY AMONG THE ILL AND ELDERLY

Hollingshead, August B. and Frederick C. Redlich, *Social Class and Mental Illness: A Community Study*, John Wiley & Sons (Science Editions, paper), New York, 1958. This pioneering study of New Haven, Connecticut, discovered significant differences among social classes in the incidence of different types of mental illness. "Each class exhibits definite types of mental illness." Psychiatric treatment was found to be relatively ineffective in treating members of lower socioeconomic groups.

Riessman, Frank, and Jerome Cohen, and Arthur Pearl (eds.), *Mental Health of the Poor: New Treatment Approaches for Low Income People*, Free Press of Glencoe, New York, 1964. This is a large and varied collection of readings appropriate to the title. It includes an article by Benjamin Pasamanick titled, "A Survey of Mental Disease in an Urban Population: Prevalence by Race and Income."

Task Force on Economic Growth and Opportunity, *Poverty: The Sick, Disabled, and Aged*, Chamber of Commerce of the United States (paper), Washington, D. C., 1965. This volume contains papers by seven experts. Some of the Task Force recommendations are controversial, for example, that all Americans 65 years of age and over should be brought into the Social Security Program.

U. S. Senate, Special Committee on Aging, *The War on Poverty as It Affects Older Americans*, Part 1—Washington, D. C.; Government Printing Office (paper), Washington, D. C., June, 1965. This is a transcript of the testimony of a dozen individuals who are concerned primarily with the condition of elderly Americans.

VI. RURAL AND REGIONAL POVERTY

Bowman, Mary Jean and W. Warren Haynes, *Resources and People in East Kentucky*, The Johns Hopkins Press, Baltimore, 1963. This research report, commissioned by Resources for the Future, Inc., offers a detailed description of the economic condition and potential of the region.

Caudill, Harry M., *Night Comes to the Cumberland: A Biography of a Depressed Area*, Little, Brown and Co. (paper), Boston, 1963. Why do the Southern mountaineers live as they do? The lure of free land pulled them into bare subsistence farming. Lumbering and coal mining provided temporarily rising income. Government relief systems now malfunction in the mountain culture. A Southern Mountain Authority is recommended as a means to replace welfare dependency with earned income.

Cochrane, Willard W., *The City Man's Guide to the Farm Problem*, University of Minnesota Press, Minneapolis, 1965. An Economic Adviser to the Secretary of Agriculture during the Kennedy years explains why there is a farm problem and what solutions various lines of action will permit. One fourth of the book is devoted to rural poverty, causes, and cures.

Committee for Economic Development, *Distressed Areas in a Growing Economy*, Committee for Economic Development (paper), New York, 1961. In this report several dozen senior executives of large corporations make 16 specific recommendations for steps to be taken to reduce high unemployment in distressed areas. Development plans and education are stressed.

Levitan, Sar A., *Federal Aid to Depressed Areas: An Evaluation of the Area Redevelopment Administration*, The Johns Hopkins Press, Baltimore, 1964. The origin of the legislation (sponsored by Senator Douglas) and the activities of the agency during its first two years, 1961 to 1963, are described in detail. The author argues for additional legislation to make the program more effective and urges continuation of government area assistance as economically justified.

Nicholls, William H., *Southern Tradition and Regional Progress*, The University of North Carolina Press, Chapel Hill, 1960. Nicholls combines psychology, sociology, and economics. The South was largely a rural slum for so long because of lack of capital and education. This author argues that growth in income requires rejection of the agrarian tradition and acceptance of industrial-urban development.

President's Appalachian Regional Commission, *Appalachia*, U. S. Government Printing Office, (paper), Washington, D. C., 1964. This report of a commission headed by Franklin D. Roosevelt, Jr., surveys the natural and human resources of the region (there are 22 tables in the statistical appendix). The Appalachian Regional Commission was created as a result of this report and was charged with the coordination of federal, state, and private efforts to develop the region.

Street, James H., *The New Revolution in the Cotton Economy,* University of North Carolina Press, Chapel Hill, 1957. Street tells why Southern cotton farmers held back from mechanization until after the Second World War, and why they finally mechanized.

U. S. Department of Agriculture, Economic Research Service, *Poverty in Rural Areas of the United States,* Agriculture Economic Report No. 63, Government Printing Office (paper), Washington, D. C., 1964. This is a statistical report on the extent and persistence of poverty in rural areas and on the socioeconomic characteristics associated with rural poverty.

Weller, Jack E., *Yesterday's People: Life in Contemporary Appalachia,* University of Kentucky Press, 1965. Weller, drawing on his 13 years of experience as a mountain minister, describes the character of a people who are not oriented upward, but who are tightly attached to small groups where success is measured by "getting along" with the group.

VII. MINORITY GROUP POVERTY

Clark, Kenneth B., *Dark Ghetto: Dilemmas of Social Power,* Harper & Row, New York, 1965. Clark set out to describe the full psychological meaning of caste segregation as experienced by Negroes in Harlem. Much of this book grew out of the author's experience with Harlem Youth Opportunities Unlimited (Haryou). The author emphasizes the weakness of the schools.

Daedalus, Journal of the American Academy of Arts and Sciences, special issues on "The Negro American," Fall 1965 and Winter 1966. Several dozen articles are included. Daniel Patrick Moynihan writes on employment, income, and the Negro family, Rashi Fein on an economic profile of the Negro American, and James Tobin on improving the status of the Negro.

Davis, John P., (ed), *The American Negro Reference Book,* Prentice-Hall, Englewood Cliffs, N. J., 1966. This book includes statistics and articles on the role of Negro Americans in economics, agriculture, history, politics, sports, and the arts.

Gans, Herbert, *The Urban Villagers: Group and Class in the Life of Italian-Americans,* Free Press of Glencoe, Inc. (paper), New York, 1962. Part of a larger research project titled, "Relocation and Mental Health: Adaptation under Stress," this study describes the culture of some 3000 Americans living in an area being levelled for urban renewal at the foot of Boston's Beacon Hill. Gans provides insight and counsel for middle-class representatives working with citizens who enjoy a way of life different from that of the middle class, and who have no desire to become like the middle class.

Glazer, Nathan, and Daniel P. Moynihan, *Beyond The Melting Pot,* M. I. T. Press and Harvard University Press (paper), Cambridge, Mass., 1964.

The Negroes, the Puerto Ricans, the Jews, the Italians, and the Irish in New York have not melted into a common culture. This book is tightly packed (and very readable) with solid information regarding the character and condition of these New York ethnic groups, especially of those members with low incomes.

Kahn, Tom, *The Economics of Equality,* League for Industrial Democracy (paper), New York, 1964. Kahn is a veteran organizer of demonstrations urging opportunities for Negroes and is presently Acting Executive Secretary of the League for Industrial Democracy (Michael Harrington is the chairman). The author favors the phrase "radical change" when urging a massive public works program and urban reorganization to provide quality education for Negro children.

Parker, Seymour and Robert J. Kleiner, *Mental Illness in the Urban Negro Community,* The Free Press, New York, 1965. The incidence of some kinds of mental illness is greater among Negroes than among whites. The authors attribute this difference to disadvantage and limited opportunity.

Pettigrew, Thomas F., *A Profile of the Negro American,* D. VanNostrand, (paper), Princeton, N. J., 1964. Pettigrew is less concerned with a profile of Negro Americans than with race relations. Psychological reactions to oppression are featured along with extended treatment of Negro American health, intelligence, and crime.

Sexton, Patricia Cayo, *Spanish Harlem,* Harper and Row, New York, 1965. Puerto Rican poverty is described as severe, but this book emphasizes the potential ability of these people to earn their way out of poverty.

Shotwell, Louisa R., *The Harvesters: The Story of the Migrant People,* Doubleday, Garden City, N. Y., 1961. The author describes the depth of poverty of these migrant workers and the reasons this poverty persists.

Silberman, Charles E., *Crisis in Black and White,* Random House (paper), New York, 1964. Silberman's cool and comprehensive analysis of the condition of Negro Americans may be the most informative book ever written regarding causes, consequences, and prospects for the condition of Negro Americans.

U. S. Commission on Civil Rights, *Equal Opportunity in Farm Programs: An Appraisal of Services Rendered by Agencies of the United States Department of Agriculture,* Government Printing Office (paper), Washington, D. C., 1965. The Commission tells how Southern whites have diverted federal aid to their own uses, while denying federal aid to Negroes.

U. S. Congress, *Voting Rights,* Hearings before the Committee on the Judiciary, United States Senate, 89th, 1st, March 23–April 5, 1965, Part 2, Government Printing Office (paper), Washington, D. C., 1965. Pages 1017–1102 are excerpts from reports of the Mississippi State Department of Education telling how the white power structure, having taxed Negroes, allocated funds to keep white schools vastly superior to Negro schools.

VIII. UNEMPLOYMENT AND
MACROECONOMIC CONSIDERATIONS

Becker, Joseph M., (ed.), *In Aid of the Unemployed,* Johns Hopkins Press, Baltimore, 1965. This is a collection of symposium papers. The papers distinguish alleviative programs (unemployment insurance, supplementary unemployment benefits, severance pay, early pensions, relief) from curative programs (the U. S. Employment Service, training, public works, and area development). The essays are by able specialists.

Burns, Arthur F., *Prosperity without Inflation,* Fordham University Press, Bronx, N. Y., 1957. Burns argues that the disadvantages of rising prices may exceed the advantages of low unemployment.

Culbertson, J. M., *Full Employment or Stagnation,* McGraw-Hill (paper), New York, 1964. Culbertson argues that the rising unemployment rates of the 1950's and the continued slack of the early 1960's were the result of federal monetary-fiscal policies. He argues for monetary-fiscal policies maintaining full employment.

Collery, Arnold, *National Income and Employment Analysis,* John Wiley and Sons (paper), New York, 1966. Collery examines the causes of unemployment and inflation, demonstrates that mass unemployment need not exist in a modern capitalist economy, and weighs the costs of policies directed toward the maintenance of prosperity.

Conference on Economic Progress, *Poverty and Deprivation in the United States,* Conference on Economic Progress (paper), Washington, D. C., 1962. The Conference represents a group of farm leaders, labor union officers, and corporation executives who, in this pamphlet, argue for vigorous Federal Government programs to reduce unemployment and promote economic growth. Poverty lines are drawn at higher income levels than by the S.S.A. There are 44 easily interpreted charts included.

Keyserling, Leon H., *Progress or Poverty, The U. S. at the Crossroads,* Conference on Economic Progress (paper), Washington, D. C., 1964. Keyserling offers a detailed statistical description of the poor and of the near-poor and urges greater federal initiative to accelerate economic growth.

Lee, Maurice W., *Toward Economic Stability,* John Wiley and Sons, New York, 1966. Lee carefully analyzes the causes and consequences of business fluctuations and the means for moderating such fluctuations.

Myrdal, Gunnar, *Challenge to Affluence,* Pantheon Books, New York, 1962, and Random House (Vintage, paper), New York, 1965. Writing at the end of the 1951 to 1960 decade of rising unemployment, the author of *An American Dilemma* argues for acceleration of economic growth to reduce unemployment and the incidence of poverty in America.

Ross, Arthur M., (ed.), *Unemployment and the American Economy,* John Wiley and Sons, New York, 1964. Seven papers presented at a 1963

University of California conference are published here along with the comments of discussants. Retraining, an expanding economy, and European experience are considered. Papers by Arthur M. Ross, Seymour L. Wolfbein, Walter H. Heller, and Otto Eckstein are included.

Wilcock, Richard C. and Walter H. Franke, *Unwanted Workers: Permanent Layoffs and Long-Term Unemployment*, Free Press of Glencoe, New York, 1963. Attention centers upon experienced workers who are permanently displaced by plant closings. Cited are the experiences of workers laid off by the closing of an appliance company in East Peoria in 1959 and of meat packing companies in East St. Louis, West Fargo, Columbus, Ohio, and Oklahoma City in 1959 and 1960. Various existing and proposed alleviating and curative measures are considered.

Wolfbein, Seymour L., *Employment, Unemployment, and Public Policy*, Random House (paper), New York, 1965. Wolfbein places the unemployment "problem" within the over-all perspective of monetary-fiscal policy that allows for employment, price, and balance-of-payments considerations. The second half of the book considers a manpower policy designed to permit the unemployed to migrate or to train for jobs at a minimal cost to the economy.

Wolfbein, Seymour L., *Employment and Unemployment in the United States: A Study of the American Labor Force*, Science Research Associates, Chicago, 1964. The Deputy Manpower Administrator, Office of Manpower, Automation, and Training, U. S. Department of Labor, describes the changing cross section of the labor force. The last chapter is devoted to the anatomy of unemployment in America since 1945.

IX. AUTOMATION AND ECONOMIC GROWTH

Asbell, Bernard, *The New Improved American*, McGraw-Hill, New York, 1963. An anecdotal survey of the effects of rising productivity. Education and training are labeled the keys to a lower incidence of poverty.

Denison, E. F., *The Sources of Economic Growth in the United States*, Committee for Economic Development (paper), New York, 1962. This is the definitive work regarding the relative importance of the various sources of economic growth in America.

Haber, William, Louis A. Ferman, and James R. Hudson, *The Impact of Technological Change*, The W. E. Upjohn Institute for Employment Research (paper), Kalamazoo, 1963. The authors provide a summary of research, examining case studies of adjustment to technological job displacement.

National Commission on Technology, Automation, and Economic Progress, *Technology and the American Economy*, Government Printing Office (paper), Washington, D. C., 1966. This report of a Presidential commission, whose membership includes Whitney Young, Jr., Thomas J. Watson, Jr., Walter P. Reuther, and Daniel Bell, is primarily concerned with arrangements by which the nation may enjoy the fruits of economic progress while minimizing the inconveniences associated with technological change.

Snider, Delbert A., *Economic Myth and Reality*, Prentice-Hall (Spectrum, paper), Englewood Cliffs, N. J., 1965. Snider puts to rest several myths, among them: "automation is a curse"; "labor unions are primarily responsible for the high standard of living of the American worker"; "although the United States has pockets of poverty, the number of impoverished people is small, and most of them are shiftless ne'er-do-wells"; and "profits are an unearned and unnecessary 'grab' on the public's purse."

X. TRANSFER PROGRAMS FOR THE RELIEF OF POVERTY

Bell, Winifred, *Aid to Dependent Children*, Columbia University Press, New York, 1965. Focusing upon the "suitable home" provision in the ADC programs of many states, the author concludes that it has been used not to protect children but to hold down the number of Negroes and illegitimate children on the caseload.

Bornet, Vaughn D., *Welfare in America*, University of Oklahoma Press, Norman, 1960. Bornet examines the changes that have taken place in America regarding the provision of welfare funds to needy groups.

Burgess, M. Elaine and Daniel O. Price, *An American Dependency Challenge*, American Public Welfare Association, Chicago, 1963. This report, a project of the Institute for Research in Social Science of the University of North Carolina, arrays a wealth of statistics, while appraising the operation of the Aid to Dependent Children program over the period 1950 to 1960.

Gordon, Margaret S., *The Economics of Welfare Policies*, Columbia University Press, 1963. Mrs. Gordon has combined economic analysis of the issues with a plea for more research and more analysis by other economists. She concentrates upon unemployment insurance and the Old-Age, Survivors, and Disability Insurance Program and their effects upon economic growth and stability. A list of 226 references is appended.

Haber, William, and Wilbur J. Cohen, *Social Security, Programs, Problems, and Policies*, Richard D. Irwin, Homewood, Illinois, 1960. This collection of 64 readings mixes analysis and description with lively controversy.

Keith-Lucas, Alan, (ed.), "Programs and Problems in Child Welfare," *The Annals*, American Academy of Political and Social Science, Philadelphia, September, 1964. This issue of *The Annals* includes 18 articles on the needs of children, on parental behavior, on ADC and other extant and suggested programs.

May, Edgar, *The Wasted Americans: Cost of Our Welfare Dilemma*, Harper and Row, New York, 1964, and New American Library (Signet, paper),

1965. May was a reporter for a Buffalo newspaper (a fact that he concealed) when he took a job as a welfare worker with the Buffalo Welfare Department to gather information for a newspaper series. Being outraged at the needs of the poor and the ineffectiveness of overburdened welfare workers, he wrote articles that won a Pulitzer Prize. In this book he writes about Newburgh, N. Y., and about the need for birth control and for welfare programs adequate to the conditions that he observed in Buffalo.

Myers, Robert J., *Social Insurance and Allied Government Programs*, Richard D. Irwin, Homewood, Illinois, 1965. The Chief Actuary of the Social Security Administration describes the operation of Old-Age, Survivors and Disability Insurance and other federal social insurance programs.

Schottland, Charles I., *The Social Security Program in the United States*, Appleton-Century-Crofts, New York, 1963. Descriptive rather than analytical, this book surveys the operation of Old-Age, Survivors and Disability Insurance, unemployment insurance, public and general assistance, workmen's compensation, railroad worker economic security programs, government employee retirement, disability sickness benefits and veterans benefits.

Theobald, Robert, *Free Men and Free Markets*, Clarkson N. Potter, New York, 1963, and Doubleday (Anchor, paper), Garden City, N. Y., 1965. Theobald argues for the need and practicality of "Basic Economic Security," a guaranteed annual income.

Theobald, Robert (ed.), *The Guaranteed Income: Next Step in Economic Evolution?*, Doubleday, Garden City, N. Y., 1966. The economy is capable of providing a guaranteed minimum income; the contributors to this collection take up the question: "Should it?"

Towle, Charlotte, *Common Human Needs*, National Association of Social Workers, New York, 1965. This is a handbook to remind middle-class individuals that they and the recipients of public assistance share human feelings that can be hurt or guided in order to help personal advancement.

U. S. Advisory Council on Social Security, *The Status of the Social Security Program and Recommendations for Its Improvement*, Government Printing Office (paper), Washington, D. C., 1965. The Council was composed of representatives from industry, organized labor, and academia. This report presents the Council's findings and recommendations with respect to the financing of the program, to coverage, and to the adequacy of benefits.

U. S. Social Security Administration, *Basic Readings in Social Security*, Government Printing Office (paper), Washington, D. C., 1960. There are 1640 references in this annotated bibliography.

XI. THE BIRTH-CONTROL CONTROVERSY

Guttmacher, Alan F., *Planning Your Family: The Complete Guide to Birth Control, Overcoming Infertility, Sterilization*, Macmillan, New York,

1964. Dr. Guttmacher is President of the Planned Parenthood Federation of America.

Monsma, John C., (ed.), *Religion and Birth Control,* Doubleday, Garden City, N. Y., 1963. The editor has assembled essays written by medical specialists for the layman. Control of conception, therapeutic abortion, and sterilization are among the subjects examined.

Ogg, Elizabeth, *A New Chapter in Family Planning,* Public Affairs Pamphlet #136C, 381 Park Avenue, New York 10016. The author asserts that each family has a right to choose whether or not it shall practice family planning. For those who choose family planning, various methods are described.

Pyle, Leo (ed.), *The Pill and Birth Regulation,* Helicon Press (paper), Baltimore, 1964. The editor has collected most of the relevant statements in the worldwide Roman Catholic debate on use of the oral contraceptive pill.

Rainwater, Lee and Carol K. Weinstein, *And The Poor Get Children: Sex, Contraception and Family Planning in The Working Class,* Quadrangle Books, Chicago, 1960. The authors report upon interviews with working-class men and women in Chicago and Cincinnati. The families interviewed tend to have more children than they wanted because the parents knew so little about birth control and have found no way to learn.

Rock, John, *The Time Has Come: A Catholic Doctor's Proposals to End the Battle over Birth Control,* Alfred A. Knopf, New York, 1963, and The Hearst Corporation (Avon, paper), New York, 1964. Dr. Rock is a Roman Catholic gynecologist who teaches at the Harvard Medical School and who was a key participant in the development of the oral contraceptive, "the pill." Here he describes that development and contends that use of the pill is moral.

XII. EDUCATING THE POOR FOR HIGHER INCOME WORK

Becker, Gary S., *Human Capital: A Theoretical and Empirical Analysis, with Special Reference to Education,* National Bureau of Economic Research, New York, 1964. The "rate of return" on investments in buildings and machines is a more familiar concept than the rate of return on educational investment in people. Becker writes about educational investment—theoretically and empirically—finding, for example, a 10% rate returned on the college entrant.

Committee for Economic Development, *Raising Low Incomes through Improved Education,* Committee for Economic Development (paper), New York, 1965. In this pamphlet a group of corporation executives makes a series of specific proposals for elementary, secondary, vocational, and adult education with the object of reducing the incidence of poverty by helping the poor to earn their way up the economic ladder.

Conant, James B., *Slums and Suburbs,* New York, McGraw-Hill Book Company, Inc., 1961, and New American Library (Signet, paper), New York, 1964. The former president of Harvard writes angrily about the inferior quality of slum schools that tend to perpetuate poverty and keep able youth of low-income families from competing with their suburban peers.

Dorfman, Robert (ed.), *Measuring Benefits of Government Investments,* Brookings Institution, Washington, D. C., 1965. Seven papers are included along with critical comment by discussants. In one paper, Burton A. Weisbrod compares the benefits with the costs of government money spent to forestall high-school dropouts.

Galbraith, John Kenneth, *The Affluent Society,* Houghton Mifflin Company, Boston, 1958, and New American Library (Mentor, paper), 1963. Book-of-the-Month Club choice, this was a best seller in the late 1950's. In this book, Professor Galbraith argues that the need for more public goods (roads, parks) exceeds the need for more private goods (tailfins) in most families. Chapters 7 and 23 consider the character of present American poverty and the desirability of investment in people to end poverty.

Isenberg, Irwin, (ed), *The Drive against Illiteracy,* H. W. Wilson Company, New York, 1964. A collection of 29 reprinted articles, the accent of this book is upon ill-education as a cause of poverty and education as a means to reduce poverty. Recently initiated programs such as Higher Horizons are given special attention. There is an eight-page bibliography.

Landes, Ruth, *Culture in American Education: Anthropological Approaches to Minority and Dominant Groups in the Schools,* John Wiley & Sons, New York, 1965. This book reports on the success of a Claremont Graduate School program to take middle-class students in teacher training out of the classrooms and into the culture of minority groups in order to improve the ability of the teachers.

McClelland, David C., *The Achieving Society,* VanNostrand, Princeton, N. J., 1961. McClelland reports on the concept of "achievement motivation," on its measurement in different cultures, and on its sources.

Ornati, Oscar, *Poverty Amid Affluence,* The Twentieth Century Fund, New York, 1966. Ornati reports on the results of a four-year study by faculty members of the New School for Social Research. Their chief conclusions are that a majority of the poor are outside the economy and that investment in people is the most effective way to reduce the incidence of poverty.

Passow, A. Harry, (ed.), *Education in Depressed Areas,* Teachers College, Columbia University, New York, 1963. This is a collection of 15 essays on the title subject.

Riessman, Frank, *The Culturally Deprived Child,* Harper & Row, New York, 1962. Riessman writes for the middle-class teachers and social workers who work with underprivileged children. This book describes the character and culture of these children. The author believes that greater middle-class understanding will permit greater lower-class accomplishment. A three-page bibliography is appended.

Schreiber, Daniel, (ed.), *The School Dropout*, National Education Association, Washington, D. C., 1964. This is a collection of 17 essays on the title subject.

Sexton, Patricia Cayo, *Education and Income: Inequalities in our Public Schools*, Viking Press, (Compass, paper), New York, 1961. Mrs. Sexton reports on Detroit schools and describes the inferior quality of buildings, equipment, and teachers provided to children of low-income families. She writes with a strong feeling of outrage.

XIII. THE WAR ON POVERTY

Coyle, David Cushman, *Breakthrough to the Great Society*, Oceana, Dobbs Ferry, N. Y., 1965. Popular political economy by an author with great faith in the poverty-reducing potential of Great Society programs.

Humphrey, Hubert H., *War on Poverty*, McGraw-Hill Book Company, New York, 1964. The Vice President states the case for federal intervention to reduce the incidence of poverty in America and he argues that the 1964 anti-poverty legislation can make a major contribution.

Office of Economic Opportunity, *Communities in Action*, U. S. Government Printing Office (paper), Washington, D. C., irregularly published periodical reporting on the War on Poverty.

Pearl, Arthur, and Frank Riessman, *New Careers for the Poor: The Nonprofessional in Human Service*, Free Press, New York, 1965. The authors argue that the poor can be trained to help other poor people in their neighborhoods.

Shriver, Sargent, *Point of the Lance*, Harper and Row (paper), New York, 1964. This book consists of a collection of speeches made by Shriver between 1956 and 1964. Some new material was added to tie the speeches together. Most of the book deals with the Peace Corps, less with the War on Poverty.

Index